THE END OF THE WORLD IS NOT YET

Israel is the key puzzle to watch Resist EU's World Government The Church must resist its Adversaries

Eugene D.M. Freeman

Printed in Victoria, BC, Canada.

ISBN: 978-1-4269-3075-1 (sc)

ISBN: 978-1-4269-3076-8 (e-book)

*Our mission is to efficiently provide the world's finest, most comprehensive book publishing
service, enabling every author to experience success. To find out how to publish your book, your
way, and have it available worldwide, visit us online at www.trafford.com*

Trafford rev. 5/19/2010

 www.trafford.com

North America & international
toll-free: 1 888 232 4444 (USA & Canada)
phone: 250 383 6864 ♦ fax: 812 355 4082

Dedication

Whosoever reads this book and receives

Jesus as his/her savior, to you and the

entire world I dedicate this book.

Acknowledgement

Glory to Jesus and the Holy Spirit for the revelation, inspiration guidance and strength given me to write this book. Certainly, I could not have accomplished the assignment, because friends and loved ones rejected the idea and were of little or no help, or encouragement. However, the Lord remained steadfast and persistent, telling me to press on and publish the revelation he gave me for his people to be informed, comforted and empowered to stand up and brave the challenges associated with propagating His eternal Gospel, so that multitude upon multitude can come to Him and be saved before the end of the world comes. For this I am superlatively grateful that Jesus could use me in this respect.

Contents

I) Jesus is alive and wants to manifest Himself to you

Believers of all strips and persuasions know that Jesus is alive. After all, the Bible records that on resurrection morning, He was first seen by Mary Magdalene who in spite of all the earthly familiarity with Jesus, failed to recognize Him, even though the angels had informed her and the women with her who brought spices to anoint His body, that he had arisen from the dead. While yet in grief, when she turned, she saw Jesus standing but thought he was the gardener. Then the Lord said to her, "Woman, why weepest thou? Whom seekest thou? She, supposing him to be the gardener, saith unto him Sir, if thou hs borne him hence, tell me where thou hast laid him, and I will take him away. Jesus saith unto her, Mary, she turned her self, and saith unto him Rabboni; which is to say, Master." (John 20: 14-16) This is the lady out of whom Jesus expelled seven demons; this very devoted sister anointed the feet of Jesus and wiped them with her hair. Is it not strange that on resurrection morning she could not distinguish Jesus from the gardener? Why? Because Jesus sometimes conceals his identity and disguises himself in manner that even his close friends, admirers, followers and disciples could not identify him. Do you remember the brothers on the road to Emmaus who were discussing the events that transpired in Jerusalem on the day Christ was crucified? Well, Jesus appeared to them and inquired about the subject of their discussion.

One of them called "Cleopas, answering said unto him, Art thou only a stranger in Jerusalem, and hast not known the things which are come to pass there in these days? And he said unto them, what things?" And they said unto Him, concerning Jesus of Nazareth, which was a prophet mighty in deed and word before God and all the people. ..how the chief priests and our rulers delivered him to be condemned to death, and have crucified him ... We trusted that it had been he which should have redeemed Israel, and beside all this, today is the third day since these things were done." (John 24:21). They further explained how the garden tomb was visited by female followers of Jesus who did not find the body there, but reported that they had seen vision of angels, but they did not see Christ. He called them fools and slow of heart, and began explaining the scripture to them. As they approached their destination, they asked the stranger to spend the night with them. They brought bread, and as the stranger broke the bread and began blessing it, the eyes of these Emmaus men opened, and they recognized Jesus. He then disappeared. They could not contain their joy, and therefore turned around and went back to Jerusalem and told the eleven disciples of Christ that they had seen the Lord. Then they also learned that Jesus had already appeared to Simon. As they discussed this strange occurrence, Jesus appeared and stood among them. He also requested for and was given "a piece of broiled fish and a honey comb" (John 24: 42). He ate natural food to prove that in deed he is not a spirit, but still a human being, the very person they all knew: walked with, talked with, etc. On a subsequent occasion, Thomas got to see the Lord, and had an opportunity to reach out and place his hand on the print left by the nails that were driven into his hands. Peter was later restored to fellowship, and Jesus walked the shores of Galilee and Jerusalem, showing himself to more than 500 people, before bodily ascending into heaven from Bethany as his disciples looked on.

Since His ascension, Christ has made several appearances to devoted believers, including the Disciple John who wrote the Book of Revelation.

Before this, Deacon Stephen, said he saw Jesus standing up in heaven as he prayed for God's mercy on those who were stoning him to death. Saul, the chief persecutor of the followers or disciples of Christ encountered the Lord Jesus as he rode to Damascus to persecute them. He was blinded, but later became a believer in Christ, got his name changed to Paul, and became an Apostle.

In modern times, we have heard many accounts of Him appearing at the bedside of the sick and healing them. Oral Roberts, Kenneth Hagen, a former Ethiopian Prime Minister as well as a prisoner who encountered Christ in prison. He was later released and became a Pastor in the City of New York. You know Jesus is still in the healing business, and he is still touching lives and regenerating sinners form damnation to eternal life.

I am also a witness that Jesus is alive. He has manifested Himself to me bodily as well. There were also times when he appeared in my vision, disguised as someone familiar or a perfect stranger. Because of this, I began referring to him as the Holy Spirit. After all, He promised to send the Comforter who will lead us in all truths, which he did in a mighty way on the day of Pentecost. Even though I know that Jesus is not the Holy Spirit, I thought it was the Holy Spirit that I would encounter on a daily basis in my Christian walk. I was wrong. One Sunday, my wife and I were riding to Church when I heard an audible voice asking me: so you say that you cannot have a destiny with someone that you cannot see?" In my heart, without speaking a word, I said no, Holy Spirit, I did not say that. Then the voice replied, "who are you calling Holy Spirit? Eugene, I am Jesus." When we arrived in Church, the Pastoral/Adoration prayer was being said. I knelt down to pray, and I saw Jesus standing before me in a beautiful beige suit steering at me. His eyes were very friendly, reassuring and comforting. He gave me a message concerning my family. This occurred in November, and by December, 2009, I began seeing Jesus more often, sensing His presence as well as hearing His voice almost daily. I just could not understand why the closeness and intimacy. Could it be that my days on earth are numbered, and the Lord is trying to reassure me, or could it just be my imagination?

He directed my attention to the Gospel of John 14:21-23—"He that hearth my commandments, and keepeth them, he it is that loveth me; and he that loveth me shall be loved of my Father, and I will love him, and will MANIFEST MYSELF TO HIM (emphasis mine). Judas saith unto him, not Iscariot, Lord, how is it that thou will manifest thyself unto us, and not unto the world? Jesus answered and said unto him, if a man loves me, he will keep my words and my Father will love him AND WE WILL COME UNTO HIM, AND MAKE OUR ABODE WITH HIM." (emphasis mine) These verses of Scripture opened my eyes and understanding to the fact that Jesus is saying that he will actually abide or dwell within us as believers. Consequently, I felt that if I continue to meditate on Him and the word of God daily, and pray regularly, He will continue to manifest Himself both spiritually as well as in the natural. My fear was therefore subsided, as I looked in anticipation of regularly encountering the Lord.

One evening, as I was watching TBN, the Lord Jesus said to me "Eugene, you have my righteousness." Then I remembered an old Methodist Hymn that my late father made us sing almost ever Sunday morning during family prayer in Liberia, West Africa. "When he shall come with trumpet sound, may I then in Him be found; dressed in His righteousness alone, faultless to stand before His throne. On Christ, the solid rock I stand, all other ground is sinking sand, all other ground is sinking sand." In essence, the Righteousness of Jesus is imputed to me, because I cannot be justified and receive eternal salvation through my own good works.

The legal theory of vicarious liability comes into sharp focus. The employer is held liable for the conduct of his servant, for tortuous acts committed within the course of executing his master's duty. Here, respondit superior, works to substitute the employer for the servant; in this case, the Creator steps forward and holds himself accountable for my sins, and pays the debt to satisfy the requirement of God's Supreme Law: "the soul that sinneth, shall die." When Christ said I have his righteousness, I understood what he meant. In deed, an exchange was made when Christ went to the cross and died for my sins and the sins of the entire world. So, God does not see me personally, when I come asking for protection, provision and forgiveness. He sees only the righteousness of Christ, and grants my petition, because I was bought with a price: the blood shared by Jesus. His precious blood took away all of my sins. Past, present and future. As the east is from the west, so far has he removed my transgressions and buried them in the sea of forgetfulness; never ever to make me answer for them. The world may try to make me recall my past, but the Lord Jesus has assured me that I do not have to live one day thinking about whatever I may have done during these many years of my earthly existence.

A word that the Lord Jesus frequently uses as I share the Gospel with others, is "regeneration." 2 Corin. 5:17 declares :"Therefore if any man be in Christ, he is a new creature, old things are passed away; behold all things are become new." The repented person is said to be quickened or spiritually recreated, thereby removing him from under the judgment of death (physical/spiritual) imposed through Adam to eternal life in Christ Jesus. "There is therefore now no condemnation to them which are in Christ Jesus, who walk not after the flesh, but after the Spirit. For the law of the Spirit of life in Christ Jesus hath made me free from the law of sin and death." (Romans 8:1-2). I always tell people to stop thinking that they can achieve eternal salvation by doing good works—animal sacrifice, praying multiple times a day, making religious pilgrimages, etc, or even by keeping the Ten Commandments or any other spiritual laws. The truth is that no body can perfectly keep any law, because even lawyers have a way of circumventing the law to safe-guard their client's interest. A lot of people, including me, have at one point in time either stolen, lied, covetted somebody's wife or property. Well, when that was done, the laws of the sovereign creator of the universe were violated, and for any breach or transgression of God's law, the penalty is death, no matter how small the violation may seem. Because mankind cannot fulfill the demands of God's perfect laws, it seems reasonable that people would take advantage of the escape provided through the atoning death of Christ, or face the consequences of eternal separation from God in this life as well as after death.

Some of the concerns that people have expressed about following Christ is that they want to enjoy their lives while they are young, and then when they are old, Jesus can take charge of them. There are two problems with this kind of thinking. Firstly, being a believer and follower of Jesus does not mean that life will be boring and meaningless. To the contrary, Jesus says that He came to give his followers abundant life (John 10:10); and He wishes that his followers/servant should prosper and enjoy good health in the natural, just as their souls prosper (3 John 2). The fact is that our salvation creates an unbreakable intimate relationship with Jesus; that is to say, you get to know Him one on one as you do your earthly parents and close relatives or friends. Such personal friendship with the savior of the world and ruler of the entire universe is priceless, because he has already paid the ultimate price, and all you have to do is receive it by faith; not by works. For it is by his grace that your salvation is assured.

On the other hand, it is the adversary, Satan, Lucifer, the devil, who as usual is determined to lead people astray; because his only purpose is to steal your joy, kill and eventually destroy you for the rest of eternity. The devil is looking for company in hell. He does not want to be there alone.

The second problem with getting old before receiving Christ is that physical death can sneak up on anybody at any time without warning. The graveyard is full with all sizes of graves, representing babies, young adults and grown ups. Death is by appointment. Hebrews 9: 27-28 beautifully clarifies this point: "..It is appointed unto men once to die, but after this the judgment. So Christ was once offered to bear the sins of many; and unto them that look for him shall he appear the second time without sin unto salvation." With my whole heart, I believe that the wisest decision that anybody could make in this life, is to receive Christ as Lord and Savior so that they can be sure about their eternal salvation. Jesus is not asking that you first repent or turn away from your sin before he can save you. He simply wants you to take a leap of faith and receive his free gift of salvation just as you are. He knows that you are incapable of forsaking your sins without his divine intervention. That is why Romans 5:8 says that God commanded his love toward us in that while we were still sinners, Christ died for us. John 3:16-17 is also on point: "For God so loved the world that he give His only begotten Son, that whosoever believes in Him shall not perish but have everlasting life. For God sent not his son to condemn the world, but that the world through him might be saved." Also in Isaiah 1:18 we find these reassuring words: "Come now, and let us reason together, saith the Lord; though your sins be as scarlet, they shall be as white as snow; though they be red like crimson, they shall be as wool."

There were times in my evangelism, I quoted John 3:18 where condemnation is pronounced for failure to believe and receive Christ. The Lord on several occasions reminded me that the emphasis should not be on condemnation, but rather mercy and grace. One night I was praying, and Jesus said to me, "prophesy of my goodness. My last name is Redeemer." Yes, it is all too easy to be judgmental, and that is exactly why some people say they are turning their backs on the Church. As agents of reconciliation, Jesus wants us to preach love, more than anything else. Does that mean we should compromise and water down the gospel, no. It simply means that we should temper justice with mercy. The letter of the law kills, but the spirit heals. Come to Jesus!

Here is a snap shot of my imperfect walk with Christ. Picture this, When the above paragraph was written, I left my computer with a prayer for Jesus to give me revelation on what to write next. This morning, as I was taking a shower for work, I began thinking about my childhood and upbringing. Something I have never done in many years. All for a sodden, the Lord said to me: " I brought you materials to complete the first section of the book. This is how divine revelation works. Receive it." I said thank you Lord, I receive it.

You see, my step-mother frequently told me stories about my Church attendance at Eliza Turner Memorial AME Church in the Republic of Liberia, where I was born. She said that I had a bow tie that I regularly wore to Church, almost every Sunday. I now recall vividly that my parents did not accompany me to Church. My father was an AME member, but he stayed home while I went to Sunday School and Church. His reason for not going was that he did not have proper clothing to wear. Because he did not want people to look down on him, he decided to stay home on Sundays. However, we usually had family Sunday Morning prayers, which he led. I may have had about two or three suits for Church, but the bow tie was an ever-present accessory. I probably went there because I wanted to show off my bow tie, just kidding. The fact is that I do not really remember any Sunday School Scripture/Lesson or any Sermon Preached by Rev. A. Benedict Mason, except that he constantly sang a Hymn that indelibly registered in my heart and on my mind throughout my childhood and adult life. I later learned the words to the song, and it states in part: "There is a fountain fill with blood drown from Emmanuel's veins, and sinners plunge beneath that flood, loose all their guilty stain ..." Another thing that the Spirit impressed on my little heart was the frequent recital of the Ten Commandments, followed by a Chant which said "Lord incline our hearts to do thy will ..." Poor Old man Ketter led the recital of the Decalogue every Sunday, probably until his death. If his righteousness was grounded in those Commandments, then I am sorry for him, because he just could not keep them. I sincerely hope he took a plunge into the cleansing fountain of Jesus' blood and received the free gift of salvation by grace. "Even the dying thieve rejoiced to see that fountain in his day" and was instantly offered redemption by Christ while still on the cross. Believe me, in all of my childlike stupidity, I asked Jesus whether the dying thieve was really in paradise with Him. His response was: "didn't I promise him that? I keep my words," He added. For his part, Rev. Mason was murdered by gunmen at his Church, the Mason Prayer Center where he was caring for some refugees during the Liberian civil war in 1989. He was faithful till death, and I am sure that he is resting in eternal bliss, because he confidently relied on the fountain of blood provided by Jesus' substitutionary death.

Let it be known that it is all too easy for a person to be a regular Church attendee, and still not be saved, and know for sure that he has eternal life. Such was the case with me. Through out the sixties and early seventies, I do not think anybody really sat me down and explained to me God's Plan of salvation. The general assumption that prevailed in Liberia was in play: every Liberian is a Christian. Consequently, people of other faiths were simply viewed as aliens. For a multiracial society as culturally diversed as America is, we know that everybody is not a Christian, and the Church has to double its efforts to win such folks, and bring them into the kingdom of Christ. And that is the primary purpose of this book.

Poor me, I thought I was a member of the AME Church, because my Father was a member. Not knowing that Jesus does not have grandchildren. Every individual who comes to Church must make that decision for himself, and when he does, Christ welcomes him into God's Kingdom as a "son" with all the rights and privileges thereto appertaining. So, I got saved when I went to boarding school, St. Andrews Episcopal School, in Cape Mount County, Liberia. I was baptized, and as a matter of policy, we attended Church every morning before school and in the evening before we went to bed. Mission life was hard. We did all kinds of physically demanding farm chores, as well as corporal punishments when we violated campus rules. When that academic year ended, I went home for vacation, at the end of which my grandfather requested for me to live with him in Fishtown, Maryland County. The reason was that I was very rebellious, and my father did not have the patience to deal with that, so he constantly used the rod of correction. My grandfather did not think that was the way to train a child, even though the Bible talks about the rod of correction. Before school reopened in March of 1964, I was living with my grandfather in Fishtown, a rural village several thousands of miles away from my parents. Grandpa was the Lay Reader of the Episcopal Church in Fishtown. He built it, and I was privileged to lead the procession and recession during Sunday Morning Divine Worship Services, holding high a wooden cross.

I saw no real effort made by anyone to evangelize the entire town. As a matter of fact, the town was divided into two sections, one area called Mission Town where Church goers and partly educated people lived, while the larger section of the Township was occupied by tribesmen with no formal western education. The Paramount Chief also lived there. People like the Township Commissioner who also taught and lived in Mission Town like us, felt more important and probably holier than those who resided in the main town. Even the Episcopal Priest who headed the Disease only came to give Communion once a month, and had no contact whatsoever with the majority of people in the Township. Witch craft and sorcery prevailed in Mission Town as well as in the main town. I recall that there were occasional disappearances of people, and the next time you heard about them, some body was confessing about the missing person being killed and eaten by the witch craft. They told stories of dead people being raised from the dead, taunted and killed for the second time and eaten. I can still remember how afraid I use to be to come outside at night to use the bathroom. A large cotton tree stood close to our house, from which an owl or group of owls use to cry or sing every night. For a person who grew up in the Capital City of Liberia, you can imagine what it was like. Had it not been for the mercy and protection of Jesus Christ, anything could have happened to me.

Grandpa Harrison was one of two Teachers that ran Fishtown Public School. During my elementary senior year (6th grade), two American Peace Corps were assigned to our school. They lived with the bulk of the villagers in the main town, at my grate granduncle's house, and were very instrumental in recruiting many children to attend school. Mr. William Post and his wife Nancy were good Teachers. They also arranged a partial scholarship for me to attend Bishop Ferguson, a boarding school owned and operated by the Episcopal Church. I was admitted in the 7th grade. There were all kinds of students from every imaginable sector of the Liberian nation. Some were children of high level Government Ministers, Directors and Managers, including the children of our then leader, President William V.S. Tubman who ruled Liberia for 27 years. Yet, there were students who came from middle income families as well as kids from the remotest part of Liberia, like myself. I got lost in the mix-up. Smoking cigarettes and drinking liquor were common in the bushes around campus. It was also easy to leave campus at night (undetected) and go downtown Harper City to party (Capital of the County in which I lived). This was something my friends and I did a lot of times. There was only one Dean of Boys, and only one Matron for the girls. Manpower was inadequate to monitor the student population. Perhaps that was why we got away with a lot of infractions, including cooking at night on campus. Some fellows may have had a key to the store room.

Emphasis was placed on religion as a means of keeping the student in check. We attended chapel every morning and evening, and the Bible was an integral part of the curriculum too. I even joined the Catechism class and got Confirmed and started taking Holy Communion. One would think that should have prevented me from smoking, drinking, fornicating and being rebellious. No, it did not. As a matter of fact, we did not see the Church leaders of our Country living exemplary lives. A lot of them were drinking and fornicating or committing adultery, like any other person who did not know better. They did not live what they preached. May be that is why Liberia had a coup d'etat in 1980. President William Tolbert and some Government Officials were killed, followed by a civil war that took the life of then President, Samuel K. Doe, along with Five Hundred Thousand plus Liberian Citizens being killed, and other displaced internally. Because of the war, many Liberians became refugees in neighboring West African Countries, as well as in the United States and Europe.

I am not playing the blame game here, knowing that I am responsible for whatever sins I committed. Today, as I look back at my past, and now know that Jesus was sitting right there by me all those many years of reckless living, I feel ashame of myself. I am also sure that he had to intervene many times to safe me from myself. Words of gratitude will not be enough to express to him my heartfelt appreciation. When I sometimes think of the kindness of Jesus towards me, my very soul cries out Hallelujah, praise God for saving me. If you think your life is beyond the reach of God, and that he does not care about you, let me declare here and now, that you are not correct. Jesus knows your condition, and is ready to deliver you from your sins. Arts 2:21 says that whosoever calls on the name of the lord shall be saved. You are no exception!

Bishop Ferguson suspended me in 1972 when my maternal Uncle, Father A.B. Collins, became Principal. Some friends and I were returning from Harper City one night, and before we could get on the bush road (bypass) to go on campus, the Dean of Boys who himself was returning to the campus that night caught us. What you need to know about the bush road is that it was frequented by ritualistic killers who would catch and kill anybody who was unfortunate. They were hunting for human organs like the heart, liver and kidneys believed to have demonic medicinal powers. Ritualistic killers extracted said organs and other body parts like the genital or tongue, and gave them to witch doctors to make good luck charms for them to get big governmental positions and wealth. These evil and ungodly practices were sometimes perpetrated by prominent people who worked in the public sector or held corporate positions. Strangely, some of the people doing such wicket acts also considered themselves Christians, and where holding positions in various Churches in Liberia. Many believed that both the coup and the civil war were God's Judgment upon Liberia. After all, Liberia was founded on Christian Principles by freed slaves from the United States of America. Is there a parallel? You be the judge.

How God spared my life and the lives of countless students who walked to and from Harper City at night remains a miracle to this very day; but you need to know that the blood of Jesus is more powerful than all the demons hell can amass and throw at Gods children, and I am a living witness.

From Bishop Ferguson I went back to my parents in Monrovia and attended Monrovia College and Industrial Training School. Upon graduating from there, I enrolled at the University of Liberia. I continued to smoke and drink during my entire undergraduate years. However, when I completed and was admitted to Law school my father died, and I had to take a hard and good look at where I was heading. I cried all night, and before the morning hours, I knelt at my bed side and recommitted my life to Jesus. I asked him to take the cigarette and liquor away from me and make me a better person. I heard no audible voice then, but the next day I did not smoke or drink, and I have remained so for almost 20 years.

I got active in street evangelism with a Christian group and later joined the First United Methodist Church where my cousin was very active in the youth group. I affiliated myself with other smaller Christian Ministries and that allowed me to spend more time in prayer and in Church, attending Bible studies and other Christ centered activities. Such programs really contributed to my spiritual growth and development. One morning, I was lying in bed tired, just waiting for day to break so I can wakeup; go to work and later to school. I had a quick vision in which Jesus appeared to me with a scroll in his hand. He was wearing a white gown with a velvet green satch across his chest. He opened the scroll and said to me, this is my will for your life; and then I got up and saw nobody in the room. I kept this to myself as a secret for a very long time. Actually, I did not think that I was going to give-up the practice of law completely for Pastoral duty. So whenever the opportunity presented itself, I did a little bit of preaching and personal evangelism; which I still do today.

By 1998, the Liberian Civil War started. I was taken behind rebel lines, and God preserved my life there; especially one day when the village that I was lodging in, with my family was invaded, and I was the only male put outside in the sun for interrogation. Armed men loyal to Mr. Charles Taylor were threatening to take me to the base at Firestone Rubber Plantation. The Twenty Third Psalm did not leave my lips, until I was released to join my family again. Conditions behind rebel lines were deplorable. There was no food or any conducive sleeping place or medical facilities. I left every thing home that morning when we were first told to leave our houses and assemble at the Omega Navigation Towers operated by the United States. I thought it would have been like the coup of 1980, when people did not have to leave their homes, especially if you were not a government official. So I left home penniless, with no change of clothes believing our stay at Omega would have been brief. I was wrong, because we were soon made to lineup and walk hundred of miles in the interior with no specific destination. We and our families stayed wherever we felt was safe. The hours became days, and the days became weeks of scavenging for food, like in the Reality Show --Survival. In our case, just one wrong turn could land you into the hands of some wicked group of rebel soldiers. Death was lurking all around the place.

By then, my entire private part had been invaded by boils, because I had only one shirt and one trousers which I worked in during the morning hours looking for food—palm nuts cassava and wild nuts to feed my family. My oldest son and I were on a constant and persistent hunt for food. Many times we returned to the village with only a bunch of palm nut or greens to eat. At night I would bath with hot water; no soap, and then put on the same dirty shirt and trousers and sleep in them. We stayed in that village for almost a month, until that province was liberated by a rival warring faction led by Mr. Prince Johnson. This made it possible for me to go to the University of Liberia New Campus –Findell, where I was treated by a Liberian Doctor who was working with Medecins Sans Frontieres. Her husband, Albert Signwuak, a classmate of mine at law school, was killed on that very campus, because he lived and worked there as a Science Instructor. Eventually, we returned home when the West African Peace Keeping Force deployed in Monrovia, and a seize fire was announced.

My law firm was reopened, and I tried ever so hard to mend my broken life. After a while, factional fighting engulfed the city of Monrovia again, and I had to leave my home and flee because a pickup load of gunmen were coming to my house. I took refuge at my cousin's house at a place called Duport Road, but after one week the rebels came looking for me, this time with my own car, a red opel sedan that they took from my house on the day that I fled. Actually, I had no where to hide. I tried going under the bed, as they began beating on the front door of the house. The bed was very low. I tried going into the closet, but concluded that it would be the first place that the armed men would search because it was close to the room door. Just in that time, the Lord spoke, saying you have not prayed yet. I recited the Twenty Third Psalm, and as I completed the last line of the Psalm, the knock on the door stopped, and then I heard the car engine. I pushed the window curtain aside, and peeped through the glass, and my car was in reverse leaving my cousin's yard. Yes, Jesus had done it for this sinner again. Give Him praise and Glory; His mercy endureth for ever and ever!! Is anyone chasing you? Keep in mind, that He who keepeth Israel, neither slumbers nor sleeps. His eyes are upon His children. Why don't you separate yourself from the carnality of this world, and surrender your life to Jesus? He will save you, friend!

I came to the United States in 1996, and by the grace of God I have been able to keep a roof over my head, doing all kinds of work below my academic qualifications to sustain myself and family, some of whom are still in Africa. Considering my age, and principally due to the difficulty in finding suitable employment, which has now gotten worse because of the recession, I have been making plans to return to Liberia to practice law. Elections were held there in 2005 and I am told that there is a semblance of stability. As part of preparation for my return, I went to Temple University's Beasley School of Law and got a Master of Laws Degree (LL.M). Because I did the program in three semesters rather than in one year, I was awarded a Degree in February, 2009. Then during the Commencement on May 23, 2009, another Degree was given to me. How someone entered my bed room and took one of my degrees away really touched my heart. I was grieving because I had suffered so much to study for my degree, and now someone just came and got it on charity. That was when the Lord manifested himself to me bodily and told me he did not appreciate the idea that I was crying over a degree. He told me who took it, and said that I should let it go, and that he wanted me to forget all about going back to Liberia to practice Law. I said ok, if you say so. Since then, the Lord has not left my side; and his presence has been real and consistently felt and his voice heard daily on a regular basis. Together we watched TBN's Christmas Pagents of December, 2009; including the crowning of "Jesus," With Jan moderating the event. I can remember standing up and praising God and waiving my hands as the gentleman who played Jesus marched towards the white throne with the long train of his purple gown dragging behind him. The Lord said: " Don't do that." But Jesus did enjoy all the Christmas programs—musical concerts, reenactments of his birth story. I recall him saying one night: "they are celebrating my birthday." Come and watch. On top of all those carefully planned and well executed programs, there were shows depicting the crucifixion. When the beating was going on, Jesus said: "a cut butt." Then as they dragged the person who played Jesus along the street with a heavy wooden cross on his back, with blood all over his body, and as they drove the nails into his hands and feet, and placed him on the cross, Jesus said to me: "I was murdered." I replied softly, for me, and he said: "yea, keep that in mind always."

I bought the DVD to Mel Gibson's Passion of the Christ when it come out, and watched it only one time. I cried so much, and I still have it among my DVDs, but I just cannot bear to watch it for the second time. Yet the Lord woke me up and made sure I watched any movie on TBN that dealt with his crucifixion. Whatever revelations he gave me during that time, and even after the Christmas, he always said: "keep it a secret. So, it was never my intention to write a book until he began telling me to publish. I really don't feel good enough to write a book about our conversations, but Jesus insisted, and because he wants the world to know that He is real, and will eventually return bodily to establish his kingdom, this book is being published to strengthen your faith, and alleviate your fears.

II) Jesus says the end is not yet

Jesus wants the Church, His followers, and the entire world to know that the end of the world is not yet, and will not be for a very long time. He says that there is still a lot to be done, because the majority of the world's population has not yet heard the gospel, and consequently there are lots of people who need to be saved and brought into His Kingdom. He wants everybody to know that His love for the world remains steadfast, and that it would be like he died in vain if a vast majority of mankind is not redeemed before the end comes. As such, Jesus is calling on His Church and individual believers to double their efforts and do the work of world evangelism, rather than to behave like the Christians of Thessalonica who became weary, stopped working and sat down with their hands folded, waiting for Christ to return. Jesus wants you to consider carefully the warning of Paul to them:

"Now we beseech you, brethren, by the coming of our Lord Jesus Christ, and by our gathering together unto him; that ye be not soon shaken in mind, or be troubled, neither by spirit, nor by word, nor by letter as from us, as that the day of Christ is at hand." Let no man deceive you by any means: for that day shall not come except there come a falling away first, and that man of sin be revealed, the son of perdition; who opposeth and exalteth himself above all that is called God, or that is worshiped; so that he as God sitteth in the temple of God, showing himself that he is God." (2 Thessalonians 2:1-4).

Thus far, we have seen many earthquakes, tsunamies, wars and rumor of wars; children against parents and verse versa, and wickedness on the increase; but we have not yet seen the man of perdition or antichrist revealed, followed by the great and final apostasy prophesied by Paul in the verses of scripture quoted supra. Nor has the Temple been rebuilt and worship therein resumed in the reconstituted Jewish State of Israel. I will revert to the issue of Israel in another chapter.

However, it is worth noting that when the disciples asked Jesus about when the end of the world would be, and what they should watch for as a sign, Jesus responded thus: "Take heed that no man deceive you. For many shall come in my name saying I am Christ; and shall deceive many … When ye therefore shall see the Abomination of Desolation, spoken of by Daniel the prophet, stand in the holy place, then let them which are in Judea flee …" (Matthew 24:4-5; 15-16).

In resent times, there has been a surge of good sermons and teachings about the rapture, and almost every Christian seems to be "praying up and packing up" for a twinkling of the eye return of Christ. The recent increased interest in the second coming of Christ to rapture the Church comes at a time when the Mayan 2012 cyclical calendar prediction is also receiving much publicity, and people all over the world are panicking. Harold Camping has also added fuel to the end time buzz by declaring that the world will end on May 23, 2011, much sooner than the Mayan calendar predicts. . There is an October 11, 2009 Article written and published on the internet by The Huffington Post on the Mayan End of the word prediction captioned, 2012: Mayan Year 2012 Stirs Apocalypse Predictions, Doomdayrs. According to the Article, even Myans in Mexico are doubting the truthfulness of the 2012 end of the world predictions, and bleam westerners for the publicity it is receiving.

What most people seem to be in agreement with is not that the Mayans foretold destruction of the world by 2012, but that a Golden Age much better than the times in which they lived would come into existence provided planet earth is cared for and treated with respect by humankind. I do not doubt that God could have given the Mayans some limited understanding or projection of future things. After all, in Genesis Chapter 41, He revealed to Pharaoh of Egypt in a dream an impending world farming, and it happened. God also used Nebuchadnezzar's dream to reveal the destruction of his kingdom, followed by the rise of future Empires and Kingdoms in the world, and some of those have been fulfilled (Daniel Chapter 2). However, Jesus has given us a better Revelation of the End of the World in the Bible, and His words can be trusted, becauses they will always come through. He washes over them to see that they are fulfilled.

Christian believers are aware that Christ said that no body knows the time when the end of the world would come, but only the Father; meaning only the Godhead, Father Son and Holy Spirit (Trinity) have absolute knowledge of escatology (end of the age), not even the Angels, who daily stand in the presence of God know when the end will be, and for any mortal: astrologer or deviner to think that he knows the exact time the world is going to end, would certainly make that person "God," which he/she is not, and will never be.We should not even be worring about the movie 2012, which beautifully uses special effects to show planes dropping out of the air and crashing into trains, buses and sky- scrapers on earth. Those that attended that movie went home perplex and afraid. ABC also talks about people in Europe and other parts of the world stocking up on every essential comodity, in preparation for the day when the world ends. I find this amusing.Rather than focusing on when the world is actually going to end, as well as how and when the rapture will occur, the Church needs to know that Jesus expects us to stand up more forcefully for the oppressed, the destitute, homeless, and victims of both natural and man made desasters. Jesus is calling on the Church to take a stand for those who have not had the opportunity to hear the gospel, and are being prevented from doing so by political leaders who want to hold them hostage under a blind repressive regime. The Lord is asking the Church to be agents of mercy, championing the cause of the unborn who are being murdered in their mother's womb everywhere in the world daily.

Jesus says that the end will not come any time soon because there are millions of people who have not been brought into the fold. To leave them hanging out their by themselves with no hope of eternal life, would make His death on the cross meaningless. In deed, the harvest is pleantiful, and that is why He, the Lord of the Harvest, will raise Up more laborers to expand the work of evangelism through out the entire world.

Therefore, hold fast and stand up for righteousness. Too often Christians become intemidated by the secular world, as well as people of other religions who are bend on silencing the Church. Everyone wants to enjoy freedom of speech and freedom of religion, but it is the Christians who are third class citizens who have no right to speak on issues affecting their societies, world and humanity at large. Christians are being killed just for practicing their faith, while it is fun to burn down churches and redicule Christ in books and movies, with some slandering Him as being the husband of Mary Magdalene whith whom He is accused of fahtering a child. Such allegations the Lord says are mere fabrications by men with senister mostives not only to make a quick buck, but also to defame and undermine His purity and devinity, and thereby reduce Him to the level of just a prophet who had extraordinary powers to perform meracles. When such things are said, the Church remains silent and does not take a strong position. Our adversaries are therefore embolden. No wonder why Pakistan and the 56-nation Organization of the Islamic Conference (OIC), have proposed an Anti Defamation of Religion Resolution to be debated and adopted by the United Nations Commission on Human Rights. This move is audacious and shameless. Pakistan, and some of the countries supporting the Anti Defamation Resolution are financing madrassas in their countries, where babies are taught and indoctrinated to become suicide bombers to kill Christians. Women in a lot of these countries do not enjoy equal rights with men, and are segregated and suppressed by their governments. One would think these are human rights violations of consequence that these countries should be correcting in their own backyard, rather than to seek to impose their Islamic laws and traditions on the rest of us who do not belong to their religion and community (Ummah).

By the way, who made the United Nations and any of its specialized agencies authority over the Church. We know only one Lord and Savior. His name is Jesus Christ, and the United Nations will not lecture or regulate how the Gospel of Jesus Christ should be propagated. I call on Christians anywhere and everywhere to resist the intrusion of the United Nations, and to disregard its Anti-Defamation Resolution in whatever form it is presented. Let me also go on record by saying that the United Nations lacks any enforcement authority for such a Resolution. It violates Feedom of Speech under the First Amendment of the United States Constitution which provides: "Congress shall make no law respecting an establishment of religion, or prohibiting the free exercise thereof; or abridging the freedom of speech, or of the press; or the right of the people peaceably to assemble, and to petition the Government for a redress of grievances." Even if the government of the United States of America were to agree to the Anti-Defamation of Religion Resolution, and ratify it in manner provided by the Constitution, it only becomes statutary law, that will not, and cannot survive when we attack it as being unconstitutional. It would require a Constitutional Amendment (See Article V of US Constitution) before any Anti- Defamation of Religion Law can take effect in America, and you show me that American Citizen or State that would allow Free Speech to be abrogated. In short, the Anti-Defamation Resolution is dead on arrival, as far as America and many other countries are concerned, and is going no where. We as Christians must stand up and be prepared to fight for our freedom of worship. We will not and should not always "turn the other cheek. " Like a mighty army, move the Church of God, brothers we are treading where the sins have trod, we are not devided, all one body we, one in hope, one in doctrine, one in charity. Onward Christian Soldier, matching as to war, with the cross of Jesus moving on before …" (From The Hymn: Onward Christian Christian Soldier). Hold fast, the end is not yet, and nobody will drive us into the sea without a stand.

"Finally, my brethren, be strong in the Lord, and in the power of his might. Put on the whole armor of God, that ye may be able to stand against the wiles of the devil. For we wrestle not against flesh and blood, but against principalities, against powers, against the rulers of the darkness of this world, against spiritual wickekdness in high places. Wherefore take unto you the whole armor of God, that ye may be able to withstand in the evil day, and having done all, to stand. Stand therefore, having your loins girt about with truth, and having on the breastplate of righteousness; and your feet shod with the preparation of the gospel of peace; above all, taking the shield of faith, wherewith ye shall be able to quench all the fiery darts of the wicked. And take the helmet of salvation, and the sword of the Spirit, which is the word of God: Praying always with all prayer and supplication in the Spirit, and watching thereunto with all perseverance and supplication for all saints."

Much is also being made of the so-called New World Order. I personally recall that when the Late President William R. Tolbert was in power in Liberia, he called for a new world order, that would provide for, and ensure equitable distribution of the wealth of the world, so that poor African and other socalled third world countries could meet the demands of technological, infrastructural and economic development. The western countries were far ahead of the rest of the world, and still are today. The appeal went unheeded, as Europe and her allies exploeted the resources of the colonies and poor nations, and resold finished products at very high prices that these countries could not afford, but had to pay because of necessity. Loans were made to their proxy governments at high interest rates. Most times, only 25% of such borried funds reached the intended countries. The remaining 75% was stolen and placed in European bank accounts, even in the Switzerland that claims to be nutural. Still, the massive debts remain unforgiven and thus continue to be a huge burden on poor countries. Diseases, malnutration, illateracy, lack of safe drinking water and medical facilities remain the order of the day. Think about the countless lives that have been lost as a result.

Previous calls for a new world order did not emphasize the creation of one world government, as is being proposed, advertised and promoted by Europe, and some Americans in academia. Does Europe think that, we Africans and Asians will relinquish our hard won sovereignty, after many years of slavelry, colonialism and neocolonialism, under the yoke of European cruel and inhumane expansion and territorial adgrandizement? Rome, Great Breatin, France, Belgum, Potogal, Spain, etc do not seem tired of repressing others. So they are creating a World Government with ten subdivisions that will include every country and continent in the whole world: North America, South America, Africa, Asia, Australia and Antarctica.

After 1945, Europe and the United States were moving heaven and earth to counter what they perceived as Soviet Expansionism, and rightly so. Communism was the greatest threat, but the Soviet Union disintegrated, and its Satellite States in Eastern Europe became free nations.

We saw the Burlin Wall and Communism falling flat to the ground, around the close of the 20th Century, and Europe is now talking about taking over the whole world? Nobody is stopping the European Union (EU) from uniting the European People, but what the rest of us decry and detest is for Europe to make all of us Europeans. It will not work now, Jesus says.

Ironically, there are Preachers who come on TBN to glorify this "New World Order" nonsense as prophetic, and would have us believe that the book of Daniel is being fulfulled. Not yet. Jesus says, this is another ploy of the enemy as they try to hasten the end time, and silence the Church even before the appointed time of the rapture and the Great Tribulation. The New World Order will not stand, and the rest of us should do all we can to resist it now.

Under the best scenario, Europe cannot succeed with its proposed World Government without the help of the United States, and even then, what do you think the Russians and the Chinese would do; sit with their hands between their legs. Really?

Much talk about President Barack Obama being the one groomed/recruited to head the New World Order or Global Government, while he was a student at Comumbia University. He is believed to have been recruited by Hon. Zbigniew Brzezinski, a former U S National Security Advisor to former President Jimmy Carter, supported by Henry Kessinger, former Secretary of State to President Richard Nixon, respectively. These people are old dogs who know no new tricks, and they cannot succeed.

Meanwhile, here is the vision I had of President Obama in mid February, 2010. He was dressed in blue shirt, blue tie, and a blue trousers, walking in the mud. Following closely behind him was something having the appearance of a dwarf; about the size of a baby carton character, about three feet tall. No other person was with the President, but the said short creature alone. When I awoke, I said what kind of dream is this? The Lord audibly spoke saying: " you are a Christian, interpretate the dream." Then I said well, the President is a Christian, and one should expect him to have Angelic Protection from the Lord? "Do you see any behind him?" The Lord asked, and I replied no. I got on my knees and began to pray for the President, and call on every American to do likewise. There is much talk about him bringing European Socialism to America, when in deed and in truth America was more socialist than a lot of Americans would like to admit, and this did not Begin on President Obama's watch.

What do you call a welfare state, with a social security program such as we have in the United States? It is certainly not what Adam Smith wrote about in his book, The Wealth of Nations. For all practical purposes, we have a mixeconomy; but do not ever thank that the Federal Government is going to take over your farms, corporations and other businesses and nationalize all of them. That would be textbook socialism, and yet you will not see the proletarit (working class) in power.

President Obama is not the "Antichrist or son of Perdiction" the scripture talks about. So, he is not the sign of the end time. Take heart, be of good courage and stand firm, the Seven Years Tribulation is not yet, and anyone who thinks that he can fake the tribulation, is joking, and should be resisted. Jesus wants his people and followers to be assured that he will come, as promised in Scripture. However, those who have rejected his blood of atonement and stand to missout on eternal life, are being given a chance to avert the curse of rejecting Jesus, so they too can be saved. Consequently, we are still some ways away from the end of the world; but Jesus says that he will not be kept waiting for a very long time.

III) Jesus Promises to keep and Protect Israel

One evening, I was watching Hal Lindsey's program on TBN. He brought up the topic of some Episcopalian Clergy calling on Israel to relinquish all of its territory and let the Arabs have the land. The Lord immediately retorted: "I will keep Israel." In deed, Israel remains an important puzzle in the end time final battle. In fact, Israel is the key single most critical sign to watch as we await the second coming of Jesus. Scripture records that Jesus will establish his throne on the mount of olives, and that His Millennium Kingdom will operate from Israel, and that He will rule the entire world for a period of a thousand years. The creation of the millennium kingdom was an integral part of the coming of Christ to earth. There were prophesies about his birth and the purpose thereof. For Example, the Prophet Isaiah prophesied in the book of Isaiah, Chapter 9:6-7 the following: For unto us a child is born, unto us a son is given, and the government shall be upon his shoulder, and his name shall be called Wonderful, Counselor, the mighty God, the everlasting Father, The Prince of Peace. Of the increase of his government and peace there shall be no end, upon the throne of David, and upon his kingdom, to order it, and to establish it with judgment and with justice from henceforth even for ever. The zeal of the Lord of hosts will perform this. Also in the Prophetic Book of Daniel we are told that the Kingdom to be established by the Lord would be for everlasting, and that it would crush all other kingdoms of the world. This is how Daniel

2:44 reads: "And in the days of these kings shall the God of heaven set up a kingdom, which shall never be destroyed: and the kingdom shall not be left to other people, but it shall break in pieces and consume all these kingdoms and it shall stand for ever."

Being colonized and repressed by Rome, the people of Israel were expecting the Messiah promised herein above, to deliver and liberate them from oppression and degradation. For them, such a Messiah would come to power and even be stronger than David who established the first Israeli Dynasty. They were not prepared for a spiritual kingdom, but rather an earthly kingdom that would get the much hated brutal Romans off their backs. But Christ first order of business was to restore the back sliden people of Israel to God, as well as reconcile the rest of humanity to the father through his death on the cross.

The signs and wonders that Jesus performed, including raising people from the dead were intended to show Israel that he is the promised Messiah, but they saw in him weakness and an unwillingness to confront the Roman occupiers, and so they rejected him, and handed him over to be crucified. All along, Jesus had said that he would die such a death and be raised from the dead, but Israel remained spiritually blind, until this very day. John Chapter 1 verse 11 confirms this rejection of Christ wherein he writes: He came to his own, and his own received him not ..."

Israel paid a heavy price for rejecting Christ. I went to bed praying that the Lord will give me material for Chapter Three of this Book, and as I lie in bed this morning, I heard the words: "Blessed is he that comes in the name of the Lord. Blessed is he that comes in the name of the Lord." The Lord repeated these words two times to show emphasis and certainty, called the double repeat in Jewish speech pattern. Then the Lord said: "read the Gospel of Luke, Chapter 19, verses 41-44, misery is prophesied in them." The Scripture reads thus: " And when he was come near, he beheld the city, and wept over it, saying, If thou hadst known, even thou, at least in this thy day, the things which belong unto thy peace, but now they are hid from thine eyes. For the days shall come upon thee, that thine enemies shall cast a trench about thee and compass thee round, and keep thee in on every side. And shall lay thee even with the ground, and thy children within thee; and they shall not leave in thee one stone upon another; because thou knewest not the time of thy visitation." Here, Jesus was making a prophetic statement about the A.D 70 conquest of Israel, and the destruction of Jerusalem and the Temple by the Romans. It happened just as he said it would. Those who barricaded in the temple kill each other because they felt that it was better for them to die, than to be taken alive in disgrace or be massacred by Roman Soldiers. Flavius Josephus, the Jewish Zealot, Pharisee and Historian confirms the life, ministry and death of Jesus, as well as the said conquest of Jerusalem in his books: 'Jewish War' and the 'Antiquities of the Jews,' respectively.

It was the events of A.D. 70 that completely dislodged and dispersed the Children of Israel all over Europe and parts of the Middle East. Israel lost the Promised Land and never existed as a Jewish kingdom/nation until 1948, after the Holocaust and World War II. The Jews have an awful experience of being slaughtered both by the Romans, and later by Hitler's Germany.

Before the days of Jesus, Israel witnessed two significant invasions and divine deportation from the land. They came because of sin, especially the sin of Idolatry. Here is the story: Scripture records that Solomon replaced his father David, and built the First Temple from materials his father left him. Solomon began having strange women, contrary to God's prohibition on marring Egyptian (Pharaoh's daughter) women, Moabites (children of Lot), Ammonites, Edomites, Zidonians, and Hittites. These women brought their Idol worship into Israel. "And he had seven hundred (700) wives, princesses, and three hundred concubines: and his wives turned away his heart. For it came to pass, when Solomon was old, … his wives turned away his heart after other gods, and his heart was not perfect with the Lord his God, as was the heart of David his father. For Solomon went after Ashtoreth the goddess of the Zidonians and after Milcom the abomination of the Ammonites. And Solomon did evil in the sight of the Lord and went not fully after the Lord as did David his father. Then did Solomon build a high place for Chemosh the abomination of Moab, in the hill that is before Jerusalem, and for Molech, the abomination of the children of Ammon. And likewise did the same for all his strange wives, which burnt incense and sacrificed unto their gods. And the Lord was angry with Solomon, because his heart was turned from the Lord God of Israel, which had appeared unto him twice. And had commanded him concerning this thing that he should not go after other gods; but he kept not that which the Lord commanded. Wherefore the Lord said unto Solomon, Forasmuch as this is done of thee, and thou has not kept my covenant and my statutes, which I have commanded thee, I will surely rend the kingdom from thee and will give it to thy servant. Notwithstanding in they days I will not do it for David they father's sake: but I will rend it out of the hand of thy son. Howbeit I will not rend away all the kingdom; but will give one tribe to thy son for David my servant's sake, and for Jerusalem's sake which I have chosen." 1 Kings 3-13.

The wisest and richest man who ever lived could not stay away from foreign women and Idol worship. After Solomon died, his son succeeded him as King, but when he took the advice of his peers over that of the elders and increased their taxes, the citizens of Israel, led by Jeroboam, rebelled against the House of David, and the Kingdom split, just as God had said; with eleven (11) tribes following Jeroboam as their King, and became the Northern Kingdom, also called Israel; that was later taken into captivity by the Assyrians in 722 B.C. (2 Kings 17:5-18).

The Tribe of Judah which remained loyal to the House of David under the Kingship of Solomon's son, Rehoboam, became known as the Southern Kingdom. It subsequently engaged in all kinds of sins, and after repeated heedless warnings given by God, in 598 B.C., Jerusalam was besieged by King Nebuchadnezzar of Babylon. He took away Jehoiachin, the King of Judah, his mother, servants and all the princes and officers, including "all the treasures of the kings' house, and cut in pieces all the vessels of gold which Solomon king of Israel had made in the temple of the Lord, as the Lord had said. And he carried away all Jerusalem, and all the princes, and all the mighty men of valor, even ten thousand captives, and all the craftsmen and smiths: none remained, save the poorest sort of the people of the land" (2 Kings 24:12-14)..

The King of Babylon installed Mattaniah, king over the remnant in Judah and changed his name to Zedekiah. After a while, Babylon's army returned under the leadership of Nebuzaradan and Jerusalem was broken down while all its fighting men fled along with King Zedekiah who was later captured; his children killed before him, and his eyes were pulled out, hands and feet bound, and he was taken to Babylon. "And he burned down the house of the Lord, and the king's house and all the houses of Jerusalem and every great man's house burnt he with fire ..." The poor people were left in the city to be vinedressers and husbandmen (herdsmen). Any vessel of value that was not taken away during the first invasion was carted away to Babylon this time. Among the people taken from Judah were the Prophet Daniel, Meschach, Abendego (names given by their captors), as well as Prophet Ezekel.

Consistent with the prophesy of Jeremiah, contained in the Book of Jeremiah 25:11-12, God made the following declarations against Judah: " ...this whole land shall be a desolation, and an astonishment; and these nations shall serve the king of Babylon seventy years. And it shall come to pass when seventy years are accomplished, that I will punish the king of

Babylon, and that nation, saith the Lord, for their iniquity, and the land of the Caldeans, and will make it perpetual desolations." 200 years prior to this, the Prophet Isaiah, named Cyrus the Great (Is. 44:21-28; 45:1, 5) of Persia (Iran) to be the person that God would raise up to destroy Babylon and free His people of Judah. It was fulfilled when Cyrus conquered Babylon, on October 12, 539 B.C. with his general Ugbaru, and made Persia the dominant empire in the ancient world; freed the Jews, and allowed them to return to Jerusalem. The Angel Gabriel also appeared bodily and revealed to Daniel that his people would return from Babylon after 70 years. (Daniel 9:24). While in captivity, Daniel also recorded many end of the world prophesies, including the life and death of Messiah (Christ):

"Know therefore and understand, that from the going forth of the commandment to restore and to build Jerusalem unto the Messiah the Prince shall be seven weeks (7 years), and threescore and two weeks; the street shall be build again, and the wall, even in troublous times. And after threescore and two weeks shall Messiah be cut off, but not for himself; and the people of the prince that shall come shall destroy the city and the sanctuary; and the end thereof shall be with a flood, and unto the end of the war desolations are determined." (Daniel 9:25-26) This piece of Scripture refers to the coming of Christ, His death for mankind, and Rome's AD 70 destruction of Israel.

The same providential grace that brought Israel out of all the captivities discussed herein above was also at work in 1948, when Israel declared her Independence, and became a nation state in the Promised Land. In spite of fierce resistance by Arab settlers who squatted on the property when Rome drove Israel out in AD 70, as Jesus prophesied, the Bible still talks about a total restoration of the Jewish People to their Historical Homeland.

34

For example, the Bible in Ezekiel 34: 11-13; 16 has these prophetic words: "For thus saith the Lord God; Behold I, even I, will both search my sheep, and seek them out. As a shepherd seeketh out his flock in the day that he is among his sheep that are scattered; so will I seek out my sheep, and will deliver them out of all places where they have been scattered in the cloudy and dark day. And I will bring them out from the people, and gather them from the countries, and will bring them to their own land, and feed them upon the mountains of Israel by the rivers, and in all the inhabited places of the country ... I will seek that which was lost, and bring again that which was driven away, and will bind up that which was broken, and will strengthen that which was sick: but I will destroy the fat and the strong; I will feed them with Judgment ..." Also in Ezekiel 37, we are taken into the valley of dry bones where we witness a prophetic spiritual restoration and resurrection of the nation of Israel that began enmasse after May 14, 1948.

Since the creation of the State of Israel, her Arab neighbours have not respected the right of the Jewish people to occupy their Historical Homeland, for which many wars have been fought to keep Israel from being over-run and destroyed. The so called "Yom Kippur War" of October 1973 is in focus. Egypt and Syria launched a surprise attack on Israel as the nation was celebrating one of its most important Religious Holidays. Jewish Tradition holds that Yom Kippur celebration causes reconciliation among people, as well as with God Almighty. This Holiday is second only to Rosh Hashanah, the Jewish New Year. That is why the Arab choose to attack on that day, because the country was in a festive mood. Arabs refer to the same war as the Ramadan War. Their attack was eventually repelled; thanks to God, American equipment, logistical, and financial support. Territories seized have been gradually returned to the Arabs. The Camp David Peace Accord negotiated between Israel and Egypt by US President Carter on September 17, 1978, helped to ease tension between the two countries, but most Muslim nations in the Middle East are determined to destroy Israel, and have not entered into peace treaties with Israel, except Jordan, again with US intervention.

Iran is now openly supporting terrorist groups Like Hamas and Hisbollah, while at the same time seeking to construct a nuclear bomb to annihilate the Jewish People and State. Iran's President, Mahmoud Ahmadinejad used the United Nations General Assembly and other public fora to deny that the Holocaust occurred. My interpretation of what the tyrant is saying is that what Hitler did to the Jews is nothing compared to what he Ahmadinejad is planning against Israel. He is actively pursuing development of nuclear weapons to be used against Israel, and has refused to submit to International oversight since he claims his nuclear program is for peaceful purposes; namely, the creation of nuclear energy. The irony of it is that Iran is the second largest oil producing country in OPEC, and could generate a lot more revenue and energy simply by building its own oil refineries, rather than rely on others to refine its oil. The truth is that Iran has no real need for nuclear energy, and is using this as a ploy to develop a bomb to be deployed against Israel. He will not succeed in this sinister enterprise, even if the western powers do nothing militarily to stop him. He knows that sanctions, no matter how strong, never work, because there are always member countries of the United Nations who are ever willing to undermine the sanctions for their selfish national interests. That was the case with Iraq's oil sanctions imposed by the United Nations as well as Blood Diamonds from Sierra Leone, West Africa.

Be at ease. Jesus who keepest Israel neither slumbers or sleep. Like Hitler's Germany, Iran will get her just recompense, even before the second coming of Christ. Salvation is of the Jews, and Jesus will honor his covenant with Abraham, Isaac, and Jacob. Apart from Abraham's descendents being the ones through whom the rest of humanity will be blessed (Genesis 12:1-3), God also made with him a land covenant: "In the same day the Lord made a covenant with Abram, saying, unto thy seed have I given this land, from the river of Egypt unto the great river, the river Euphrates, The Kenites, and the Kenizzites and the Kadmonites, and the Hittites, and the Perizzites, and the Rephaim, and the Amorites, and the Canaanites, and the Girgashites, and the Jebusites."Genesis 15:18-21). Later in Genesis Chapter 17 God appeared to Abram, and instituted circumcision as the sign and confirmation of their covenant, and changed his name to Abraham; promised to make him fruitful, and that nations and kings shall come out of Abraham. "And I will establish my covenant between me and thee and thy seed after thee in their generations for an everlasting covenant, to be a God unto thee, and to thy seed after thee. And I will give unto thee and to thy seed after thee, the land wherein thou are a stranger, all the land of Canaan, for an everlasting possession; and I will be their God." (Genesis 17:7-8).

Christ is also the fulfillment of that aspect of the Abrahamic covenant that relates to all of the families of the earth being blessed. By his vicarious (substitutionary) death on the Roman Cross at Calvary, His resurrection and ascension into heaven, we the Church, principally comprised of gentiles have been grafted (Romans 11:15-17) into the Abrahamic covenant, and made partakers with Israel in the blessings of the Abrahamic Covenant. The Apostle Paul carries this "concept of adoption" further and more forcefully, and explains it in Galatians Chapter Three (3). Because of space we will not go into detail here.

Suffice it to say, however, that the land portion of the Abrahamic covenant belongs to the seed of Abraham's body, through the son of promise—Isaac, whose direct descendents are accounted for through Jacob, known as Israel (a Prince of God). Contrary to what some Theologians are teaching, the Church has not replaced Israel. God has a separate plan for Israel which is tied to the land covenant, while His plan for the Church relates to the heavenly Kingdom. That is why the Church will be raptured, while Israel goes through the Great Tribulation.

The current war in the Middle East is a spiritual war in which people opposed to God's sovereign will continue to deny and deprive Israel of the peaceful possession, use and enjoyment of its legitimate real property—the land of Canaan. Concessions have been made with the Palestinians for the sake of peace, even though they are not the rightful owners of the land. The people who now call themselves Palestinians are descendants of Arabs who occupied the area principally after AD 70 when Rome drove Israel out. Joseph E. Katz, a Middle Eastern Political, Religious and History Analyst, wrote and published on the internet a good historical analysis of the origin of the name Palestine and Palestinians. According to him, these names refer to the Philistines (Falalstin) mentioned in the Bible. They were of Asia Minor and Greek origins, not Arabs.

The Romans who drove Israel from their homeland, in 70 A.D. adopted these names to obliterate any and all Israeli historical identity or ties with the land of Canaan. Jews were taken to Rome in large numbers, and used as slaves to construct the coliseums in Rome. While away, Arabs from various places in the Middle East converged upon and took over the promised land of Israel, and stayed there until Rome fell in 476 A.D, and was replaced by the Ottoman Empire of Turkey.

The Ottoman Empire met the Arabs living in Israel, including Bethlehem, where Christ was born. This Empire was dislodged by the British around 1917, who became dominant power in the region. By the end of World War One, the League of Nations formerly placed the territory under British Mandate around June 1922. The historical homeland of Israel was a British Protectorate when Jews began returning there, principally after World War Two. Various Christian Organizations and Churches in England and other parts of Europe and America, facilitated the process.

During an interview Pastor Benny Hinn recently had on TBN with an Israeli Foreign Ministry Official in March, 2010, he (the Official) confirmed the Roman plan to change the name of Israel to Palestine. Describing the Palestinians occupation of Israel to be like a person coming from a long trip and meeting squatters in his house, the Official indicated that the homeowner then allowed the squatters to remain in a portion of the house, but the squatters became ungrateful and started to demand that they be placed in exclusive possession of the entire house. Exactly! This is the nature of the Israeli Palestinian conflict.

These facts are well documented, yet, the international community is pressing Israel to cede more territory to the so called Palestinian People. Whatever land they have been given in the past they have used as a lunch pad to fire rockets into Israel. Suicide bombers they have also sent to disrupt the Jewish nation and kill its citizens, and there are those who believe that Israel should not exercise the right of self-defense? If the Palestinians are using the current territory given to them for terrorist attacks on Israel, where is the wisdom and logic for giving them statehood that will legitimize their purchase of whatever weaponry they can afford to buy or manufacture? This goes to the heart of the stupidity of United Nations and every other nation that advocates a two state solution as a basis for lasting peace between Israel and the Palestinians. History has shown that the more territory Israel gave to the Palestinians, the more they have requested, and they will not rest until their declared objective of driving Israel into the sea and from the land is accomplished, even though they already have Jordan with seventy percent (70) of its population being Palestinians. What more do they want? Only trouble, death and destruction.God forbid, their plan will never succeed.

Palestinians have constructed the Dome of the Rock and Al Aqsa Mosque on the very Temple Mount where Herod's Temple stood in the days of Jesus, and they are now calling for the partition of Jerusalem, the Eternal City of Israel, to become the Palestinian Capital if they are granted statehood. Jesus is opposed to this, and he reaffirmed to me in a double repeat: "Israel, Israel I will protect and keep."

Before Christ returns to subdue the Anti-Christ and establish His Millennium Kingdom in Jerusalem, the Jewish people must exercise their Legal and International right to self-defense, and protect their God given Homeland. Be comforted also, that until the Church is raptured from this earth, we will continue to pray for Israel and do whatever it takes in any court of law and in any capitol of the world, to ensure that Israel is not pressured into signing any peace accord that does not uphold and preserve its Historical Identity. It is about time that we radicalize the Church once again as did the Apostles and other first Century Christians whose blood watered the seeds of the Gospel. Christians must Participate in their national governments, as well as any and all international organizations as well as community groups that affect the lives of God's people every where. We must be fruitful and subdue the earth in its entirety.

All End Time Prophesies contained in the Books of Ezekel, Daniel and Revelation, respectively point to the fact that Messiah Christ Jesus would eventually establish a 1000 year Kingdom on the earth and rule the world from Israel, at the end of the Great Tribulation. There is an abundance of literature by Biblical Scholars devoted to these Prophesies, which include the Rapture of the Church, the Mark of the Beast, deeds of the expected Anti-Christ, as well as the Battle of Armageddon in which Jesus will defeat the Anti-Christ. I do not wish to add more to such good scholar expositions, except to say that God says what he means and means what he says. The entire world will witness a literal fulfillment of these prophesies, as was done with other Biblical Prophesies, and attempts by any nation or group of nations to short circuit, circumvent and preempt Gods Sovereign End Time Plan by creating any kind of World Government or New World Order, will soon realize that they are only kicking against the pricks, and that they will not and cannot succeed. Friends, Jesus says the end is not yet!

IV Jesus debunks myths and legends

The internet abounds with all kinds of ancient myths and legends about certain artifacts said to be associated with Jesus. These include the Shroud of Turin, The Holy Grail and the Bethlehem Star that guided wisemen to the birth place of Jesus. The Lord has declared all such myths untrue and mere fabrications by people seeking fame and fortune.

A) Jesus Says Shroud of Turin is not genuine

I was watching TBN one night, probably about 1 or 2 a.m. in December, 2009 when a program about the Shroud of Turin came on. I was impressed by the science behind it, but decided to inquire of the Lord by prayer (while still watching the documentary), whether The Shroud of Turin is genuine and authentic? Jesus clearly spoke to me saying "it is a fake." The documentary was aired for the second time another night, when the Lord again declared the Shroud not authentic, and commanded me to write about this that Christians may know the certainty of the issue, since a lot of us are carried away by such myths.

What is the Shroud of Turin? IT is believed to be the cloth in which the body of Jesus was wrapped and buried that made its way from Jerusalem through Turkey and then to Turin, Italy. A piece of cloth in which his head was said to have been wrapped, bears an imprint of a human face, believed to have been imbedded and formed by the light that emanated from his face during his resurrection from the tomb.

The Gospel of John presents a good picture of the condition in which he and Simon Peter saw the burial cloth when Jesus left the Garden Tomb on resurrection morning: "So they ran both together and the other disciple did outrun Peter, and came first to the sepulcher. And he stooping down, and looking in, saw the linen clothes lying; yet went he not in. Then cometh Simon Peter following him, and went into the sepulcher, and seeth the linen clothes lie, and the napkin, that was about his head, not lying with the linen clothes, but wrapped together in a place by itself. Then went in also that other disciple, which came first, and he saw and believed."

No where in scripture are we told what became of the burial clothes; whether they were removed by the Disciples, Mary Magdalene or the Roman guards who reported to the authorities that Jesus' body had been stolen. On point is an Article written by National Geographic Daily News entitled: Shroud of Turin Not Jesus' Tomb Discovery Suggests. The Article was written by Mati Milstein in Jerusalem, and updated December 17, 2009. Thousands of ancient tombs around Jerusalem were reportedly opened and investigated, including the tomb where the current Shourd of Turin allegedly originated. Contrary to Jewish custom of transferring the skeletal remains to a bone box, it was reported that a body was found in the Tomb. The Shroud from that body is the one said to be Jesus' and that the result of the carbon dating done on it is misleading because of the amount of heat it was subjected to, having been sealed for more than a century.

However, we are aware that Jesus arose from the garden tomb. His Disciples were informed, and when Peter and John arrived at the tomb, they saw the head piece neatly folded and placed on a slab, while the coagulated (by spices and myrrh) swaddling or gauzelike grave clothes was lying at the bottom of the tomb. His Disciples did not remove these items. It is legical to conclude that both the cloth that Jesus' face was covered with, and the grave clothes that his body was wrapped in, were removed from the tomb by the Roman Guards and destroyed probably by burning to destroy evidence of Jesus' bodily resurrection, and thereby authenticate their lies to the Highpriest that Jesus' body was stolen by his Disciples while the Guards were sleeping. The Highpriest and Elders of Israel gave the Roman Guards a large sum of money to continue telling this lie and also promised to protect them from Pilate (Matt. 28: 11-15). What the soldiers and the Highpriest did not know is that the tomb had already been inspected by followers of Jesus, before the soldiers returned to the tomb and removed the grave clotes and head piece for destruction and/or concealment.

The Roman Soldiers had a vested interest in doing what they did, because their lives were at stake, and had they not gotten the cooperation of the Highpriest to intervene, as he did, all sixteen of those solders who guarded the tomb of Christ would have been put to death for "sleeping on guard duty." That was the punishment given to a Roman Soldier for sleeping on duty. How could sixeen Roman Soldiers go to sleep at once, and not hear someone rolling such a big stone away from the tomb. The noise alone would have been enough to wake all of them up, had it been the Disciples tampering with the seal and stone that covered the tomb. It took a miracle of God to roll away the stone on that resurrection morning, and nobody knows how the stone and the soldiers were removed from the enterence of the tomb, but the empty tomb is still in Jerusalem on display, and thousand of people have seen it.

Moreover, with the exception of John the beloved, all the other Disciples were afraid, and like Peter, remained in hiding during the entire crucifixion, and could not have been brave enough to go to the tomb at night in the presence of trained Roman Soldiers and break the Roman Seal that was placed on the stone covering of the tomb. As such, we are left to believe, and based on the weight of eye witnesses account, that Jesus arose from the dead bodily, and continues to live sicne his well attended ascension into heaven. The Lord told me that the Shroud of Turin is a fake and I believe His word.

45

The legend of the Shroud lives on, and I would think it is a tool in the hands of satin to mislead and divert our attention from the fact that simply calling the name of JESUS in the time of illness or any trouble is enough to summon all the powers of heaven into the caller's direction. Jesus Further declared that All powers, in Heaven and on Earth is given to him, and in it we should go out and preach the Gospel, teach and baptize those who believe. For there is no other name given in Heaven and on Earth by which mankind can be saved; and that whenever the name of Jesus is called, every knee shall bow and every tongue shall confess both in Heaven and on Earth that Jesus is Lord. We are commanded to pray in His name and ask for whatsoever we desire in his NAME, not a piece of cloth or any other presumed relic of the past. Do not be deceived! Our adversary the devil is at work promoting the Shroud of Turin. Reject it because the Lord says it is not genuine.

B) Jesus says the Holy Grail does not exist

TBN aired a documentary on the Holy Grail in December 2009, and as usual, I was watching; because most times the Lord keeps me up watching TBN, and even when I begin to fall at sleep, he would say wake up or make a sound or send a jolt of Holy Ghost Power like a thunder bolt through my body, and I would open my eyes. Such was the case on the night that said program was shown on TBN, and the Lord said to me in an audible voice, "the Grail does not exist." I asked, is that right, and he replied, "yes!"

The word Grail comes from the Latin word gradale, which is a vessel used to bring additional food or drink to the table between courses of a meal. It is shaped like a cup, goblet or chalice that the Catholics, Episcopalians bless and drink the wine from during Communion. The Lord Jesus and his Disciples are believed to have drunk from the Holy Grail on the night that he instituted or established the Holy Communion in the Upper Room. It is said that Joseph of Arimathea who requested Jesus' body from Palite, drained the blood and sweat of Jesus into said Communion Cup that he drank from in the Upper Room, as he and Nicodaemus rubbed His body with spices, and wrapped it up for burial in Arimathea's personal tomb that he provided for the burial of Jesus. Joseph was a rich man, a Counselor of the Sanhedrin that staged the mock late night trial at which Jesus was condemned or found guilty of Blasphemy under Jewish Law, but later handed over to the Roman authority with a charge of treason for proclaiming Himself King of the Jews; an offence that carries the death penalty by crucifixion under Roman Law. Necodamus was a Sanhedrin member as well, the Pharisee that came to Jesus by night asking how he could obtain eternal life; and Jesus told him that he had to be born again of water and of the Spirit; failing which he could not enter the kingdom of heaven; for that which is born of the flesh is flesh, and that which is born of the Spirit is Spirit (See John 3:1-15). This Nicodemus who was afraid to be seen by his fellow Pharisees following Jesus by day, was the very one who became bold and asked the Sanhedrin why, contrary to Jewish Law, were they condemning Jesus without first hearing the evidence? Yes, he was at the tomb applying spices to Jesus' body, because the next day fell on Saturday, the Sabbath, and the body could not be kept much longer. Purification Day for the Passover was at hand (See John 19:14, 31).

Matthew puts it this way in his Gospel: "When the even was come, there came a rich man of Arimaathea, named Joseph, who also himself was Jesus' disciple. He went to Pilate and begged the body of Jesus. Then Pilate commanded the body to be delivered. And when Joseph had taken the body, he wrapped it in a clean linen cloth, and laid it in his own new tomb, which he had hewn out in the rock: and he rolled a great stone to the door of the sepulcher, and departed (Matthew 27:57-60).

After the death of Jesus, Joseph of Arimathea is said to have been imprisoned for a protracted period of time, and the Holy Grail provided fresh water daily for him to drink. He was sustained in prison by it, and when he fled to Britain, settled with his family members and followers in Ynys Witrin (Glastonbury), but the Grail was taken to Corbenic and placed in the Great Castle of Corbenic, and guided by Grail Knights. Legend say the castle disappeared for a very long time, and when it was discovered, a descendent of Joseph, by the name of Galahad was allowed to have the Grail, and it later took him to Heaven, because it made him pure and sinless.

When the name of Joseph of Arimathea was first mentioned in the TBN documentary, the Lord audibly said: "He had clout." However, Jesus said the Holy Grail does not exist, and that people are making up these stories to make money and undermine the Church as a whole.

Regarding the Holy Communion, the Lord said to me that "anybody who rejects his blood is cursed." Christians still eat the Lord's Supper since He established it in the Upper Room. It has become a doctrinal issue too, nevertheless, it is celebrated and drunk in grails, goblets or glasses of all kinds and shape. Here are some teachings on the Communion.

The Catholic Church believes in Transubstantiation, a doctrine in their Catechism which holds that the wine and bread become the actual blood and body of Jesus when blessed by the Priest during Mass. Therefore, the Mass is central to Catholic worship, and they eat Communion every day at Mass. Only the Catholic Priest drinks the wine in the cup called a Chalice. The rest of the congregation only eats the bread but believes that it has also fully taken part in the entire Eucharist.

The Lutheran Church believes in Consubstantiation. Its founder, Martin Luther who started the Protestant Reformation, differed with the Catholics, and held that Christ is actually present in the Communion bread and wine, and that it undergoes no transformation.

Most Reformed or Protestant Churches simply believe that the bread and wine are symbolic of Jesus' body and blood, and that we partake of

Holy Communion in remembrance of Him and His broken and bleeding body on the cross when he was crucified, and died to cleanse and forgive our sins. Protestants/Pentecostals are no longer waiting for the usual First and Third Sunday Communion Services before eating Communion. They now bless their own individual Communion at home and eat it every day for healing and spiritual growth and cleansing. I am joining the band wagon, having received a Communion set from TBN, the only station that the Lord now allows me to watch.

Here is what Matthew 26:24-29 say about the Lord's Supper: "The Son of man goeth as it is written of him: but woe unto that man by whom the Son of man is betrayed! It had been good for that man if he had not been born. Then Judas, which betrayed him, answered and said Master, is it I? He said unto him Thou hast said. And as they were eating, Jesus took bread, and blessed it, and broke it, and gave it to the disciples, and said, Take, heart; this is my body. And he took the cup, and gave thanks, and gave it to them, saying, Drink ye all of it; for this is my blood of the new testament, which is shed for many for the remission of sins. But I say unto you, I will not drink henceforth of this fruit of the vine, until that day when I drink it new with you in my Father's kingdom."

In the Gospel of Luke 22:19 we find these words: "And he took bread, and gave thanks, and brake it, and gave unto them, saying, this is my blood which is given for you, this do in remembrance of me"

Paul, addressing the misuse of the Communion by some in the Church of Corinth, wrote these words: "Wherefore whosoever shall eat this bread, and drink this cup of the Lord, unworthily, shall be guilty of the body and blood of the Lord. But let a man examine himself, and so let him eat of that bread, and drink of that cup. For he that eateth and drinketh unworthily, eateth and drinketh damnation to himself, not discerning the Lord's body. For this cause many are weak and sickly among you and many sleep. For if we would judge ourselves, we should not be judged. But when we are judged, we are chastened of the Lord, that we should not be condemned with the world. Wherefore, my brethren, when ye come together to eat, tarry one for another. And if any man hunger, let him eat at home; that ye come not together unto condemnation."

In essence, whether you believe that the actual body and blood of Jesus are present in the bread and wine, or you are just eating it in remembrance of Christ, just be careful how you eat Communion. One way is to confess all known sins and ask for God's forgiveness. Also try to make peace with your enemy and or neighbor before partaking of the Lord's Supper; because the Communion is symbolic of the death of Jesus to reconcile fallen man with God.

Unlike the Catholics and Episcopalians, most Churches have departed from the goblet, chalice or "grail." Communion is served in small individual glasses most times in a round try. Some attribute this development to the need to prevent diseases, since drinking from one cup/goblet could pass germs from one person to another. Whatever! We need to know that the communion binds us as one body united in Christ, irrespective of doctrinal differences. In effect, what we have is unity in diversity, yet made and redeemed of one blood.

As for the so called Holy Grail, you need to remember what happened to Belshazzar and the top officials of Babylon when he ordered the golden and silver vessels or grail that were taken from Solomon Temple to be brought into the ballroom for he King Belshazzar (son of Nebuchadnezzar) and his princes and guests to drink wine from, as they praised their gods of gold, silver, brass, iron, wood and stone. Suddenly appeared "a man's hand, and wrote over against the candlestick upon the plaster of the wall of the king's palace: and the king saw the part of the hand that wrote." (Daniel 4:5) These are the words that the hand wrote in Hebrew: "Mene, Mene, Tekel, Upharsin." Strange words that no Babylonian astrologers or soothsayers could interpret. The Prophet Daniel was sent for and he gave the meaning: "Mene; God hath numbered thy kingdom, and finished it, Tekkel; thou art weighed in the balances, and art found wanting. Peres; thy kingdom is divided, and given to the Medes and Persians." (Daniel5:25-28)

That very night, the army of Cyrus encircled Babylon and slaughtered King Belshazar and all of his men. That is how God dealt with Babylon for desecrating his Holy Vessels.

So the current fascination with supposedly "Holy Grail" is nothing new, but just remember that Jesus disapproves of the prominence and publicity this falsehood is being given. Let me conclude this phase by empatically stating that there are people all over the world who have received healing and spiritual renewal from the Holy Communion, irrespective of what it is served in, and Christian should not place their faith in any so called "Holy Grail" out there.

C) Planet Saturn was the Bethlehem Star

The Lord and I also watched a program about the Bethlehem Star that shone so brightly over the manger when Jesus was born in Judea. The Astrologer who did the story said that Jupiter and Mass were the two stars that combined their lights into one. This is known as conjunction, or gathering of planets, which is said to be impossible that they would shine as one star.

Jesus told me it was the Planet Saturn that served as the Bethlehem Star by which the Magi were led, not Jupiter and Mass. Some Theologians have said that it was the Chicaner Glory that shone, like the glory of the lord that Moses saw on Mount Sinai, or the light that blinded Saul's eyes. Of significance is the fact that Scripture says that Jesus is the Light of the world, as well as the light that lightens every man that comes into the world. Jesus calls on us to let our light so shine that men may see our good works and glorify our heavenly father. Sadly, many of us have lit the light and placed it under the bed, in stead of putting it on the lamp stand for it to brighten the entire room.

The Bethlehem star was a symbol pointing to baby Jesus as the light of God that would lighten this dark and sinful world. That Star called on men to desist from walking in darkness, have their minds renewed and refocused in the direction of God. However, the historical records show that people are not coming to the light because their deeds are evil, and this is what the Lord Jesus wants to change, because in him is no darkness or shadow of turning. You have already seen and heard of Jesus, the true and living star of Bethlehem. Why don't you drop whatever you are currently occupied with, and come to him, like the Magi from the east who traveled several miles just to see and worship the King of Kings and present him valuable gifts. You could begin by unconditionally surrendering your life to Christ, and He will make the difference that you so desire.

V) Overview of Some Divisive Christian Theological Doctrines

The Church is one body, with Jesus Christ as the head. In spite of this unity, we are diverse, based on interpretation of Scripture, Worship and Administration. In This Chapter, we will look at some of the Theological Doctrines that account for our diversity, and perceived divisiveness.

A) The Existence of God

The existence of God is only known from the presupposition that God exist and that He has revealed Himself in the Bible and in Christ. The Universe also reveals God's existence but the knowledge of God that we get from the universe is tainted by the fallen nature of man. As such, we cannot get a perfect understanding of God's existence from observing the stars, sun, moon, planets, rivers, oceans and landforms. These things do not reveal God as much as Scripture does, even though they display his creative power.

Scripture declares that no man has seen God, but the Son, Jesus Christ has revealed Him. According to Berkhof, the presupposition of God's existence is definite. "The assumption is not merely that there is something, some idea or ideal, some power or purposeful tendency, to which the name God may be applied, but that there is a self-existent, self-conscious, personal being, who is the origin of all things, who transcends His entire creation, but is at the same time immanent in every part of it. (" Louis Berkhof, Systematic Theology, New Combined Edition, William B. Eerdmans Publishing Company, Grand Rapids Michigan/Cambridge, U.K., 1996, pp. 20-21)

This knowledge of the existence of God can only be received and accepted in faith. Such faith is not a blind and misplaced belief. Rather, it is reliably grounded in the Bible, God's infallible word. Hebrews 11:6 states: "But without faith it is impossible to please Him; for he that cometh to God must believe that he is, and that he is a rewarder of them that diligently seek Him."

However, man has developed philosophical concepts to explain or justify the existence of God:

(1) The Ontological Argument holds that man innately has an idea of the Existence of an absolute being.

(2) The Cosmological Argument states that there is a cause for Everything in the universe. So, there exists God. Taken to its logical Conclusion, this assertion denies the self-existence of God.

(3) The Teleological Argument which contends that the universe shows Intelligence, order, harmony and purpose. So by analogy, there exist an Intelligent purposeful being.

(4) The Moral Argument assumes that there is a lawgiver and judge in the Universe. So there exist a supreme being.

(5) The Historical or Ethnological Argument asserts that amongst all Peoples and tribes on earth, there is a sense of the divine (Ibid, p. 26-27).

As appealing as these arguments are, they do not reflect the Christian Theological view for the existence of God. Our explanation for God's existence is inductive. It comes from evidence contained in the Holy Scripture. It is not deductively derived from observing the universe. It is not a product of guesswork or speculation. Rather, it comes from our faith in God's word, knowing that He does not lie.

Knowability of God

Martin Luther refers to God as being both hidden and revealed. John Calvin states that even though God can be known from his revelation contained in the pages of Scripture, as well as in the person of Christ yet, the full essence of God is incomprehensible (Ibid, p. 29).

Thus, the Christian Church teaches that God is incomprehensible, but knowable. This knowledge of God is an indispensable prerequisite for salvation. In John 17:3, Christ declared: " …This is life eternal, that they might know thee the only true God, and Jesus Christ whom thou has sent." Also, in John 14:21 Christ proclaimed: " He that hath my commandments and keep them, he it is that loves me; and he that loves me shall be loved of my father, and I will love him, and will manifest myself to him." Further, in John 1:18 we read this: "No man hath seen God at any time; the only begotten Son, who is in the bosom of the Father, He hath declared Him." In deed, God is knowable.

The knowability of God is divided into two parts. (1) Special revelation-which is the revelation of God in Christ and in Scripture. (2) General Revelation-which is the knowledge of God gained from his masterful creation of the universe.

According to Scholasticism, natural revelation provided the necessary data for construction of a scientific natural theology by human reason. However, doctrines such as The Trinity, the incarnation and redemption are provided by special revelation in the Scriptures. (Ibid-p. 37)

According to Bath, there is no revelation in nature. That revelation never exists on any horizontal line but always comes down perpendicularly from above. He contends that only he who knows Christ knows anything about revelation at all. This revelation, Bath says, is an act of grace, by which man becomes conscious of his sinful condition, but also of God's free, unmerited, and forgiving condensation in Jesus Christ (Ibid).

Secular philosophers have denied the knowability of God. Their primary contention is that the human mind is incapable of knowing anything that exceeds the capability of his thinking faculties. Holders of this view include agnostics. Hume is considered the father of modern agnosticism. He did not out rightly deny the existence of God, but believed that man cannot acquire true knowledge of His attributes. (Ibid, pp. 30-31) Practical and Theoretical atheist also deny the knowability of God as well as his existence.

In summary, it is God who communicates knowledge of Himself to man. However, man cannot comprehend God in His totality. To do so, would make man God; but the revelations that God has given man are adequate enough to bring mankind to salvation in Christ Jesus.

Names of God

The names of God are not inventions of man. They are directly given by God Himself, reflecting the manner of His interactions with mankind. Berkhof says the name of God is His self-revelation even though they are all derived from human languages? They contain, in a substantial way, the revelation of the Divine Being, though not the totality of His Divine essence.

Below are some of the revealed names of God that are recorded in Scripture:

(1). EL ELOHIM and ELYON. The preface EL is the simplest name given to Israel in the Old Testament. It connotes that God is strong and mighty. ELOHIM (Him is plural in the Hebrew language) shows God as the mighty one; an object of fear. It indicates fullness of power. The name ELYON means to go up. Thus God is the high and exalted one. Transcendence is hereby implied. When Melchizedek, Priest and King of Salem blessed Abraham, he said " ...Blessed by Abraham of the most high God, possessor of heaven and earth." Gen. 14:19.

(2). ADONAI- By this name God is regarded as the lawgiver and supreme judge and ruler of the entire universe, to whom every thing is subject, including mankind. Here, God is the transcendent. Another application of this name is Jehovah (Yahweh)

(3). SHADDAI and EL-SHADDAI – By this name, God is the All powerful in heaven and on earth. On the day of His ascension into heaven, Jesus declared to his disciples: "All power is given unto me in heaven and on earth." Matt. 28:18. In effect, Christ was saying I am EL-SHADDAI. In this name, God is presented as the source of all spiritual blessings and comfort. In the Old Testament time God appeared to Abraham by this identical Name in Ex. 6:3- " ...I appeared unto Abraham, Isaac and unto Jacob by the name of God Almighty, but by my name Jehovah was I not known to them." Further in Ex. 6:4 we find "And I have also established my covenant with them to give them the land of Canaan, the land of the pilgrimage, wherein they were strangers." The imposition of covenants by God in the name EL-SHADDAI strongly signifies his Sovereign power and will to perform every contract He enters into with His people. Thus, when Christ told His disciples to go unto all Nations and teach and baptize in the name of the Father, Son and Holy Spirit, promising He would be with them always Even unto the end of the world, He was also affirming that He has the power to make them accomplish the great commission.

(4) YAHWEH and YAHWEH TSEBHAOTH- In the name Yahweh, Berkhof says God revealed Himself to Israel as the God of Grace. It is regarded as the most sacred and the most distinctive name of God that bears His Communicable attribute of grace. Dread of this name by Jews caused them to substitute it with either Adonai or Elohim. The name Yahweh Tsebhaoth carries the following Meaning:

> (a) God is the Head of the armies of Israel.
> (b) God is the head of the host of Angels. (c) God is the head of the Stars. Thus, Yahweh Tsebhaoth expresses the glory of God as King. (Berkhof, <u>Systemmatic Theology</u>, p. 50).

A review of the New Testament reveals the following names of God:

> (1). Theos- It is the Greek word for God. It represents a translation of the Old Testament Hebrew names of God. For El Elohim and Elyon the Greek New Testament refers to God as Theos. It expresses essential deity. The Hebrew 'Elyon is rendered by the Greek: Hupsistos in Mark 5:7, Luke 1:32, 35, 75; as well as in Acts 7:48.

> (2). KURIOS – This Greek New Testament name of God is the same as Yahweh as well as Alpha and Omega. Kurios is said to be a derivative of the Greek word Kuros, which means power. It designates God as the mighty one, the Lord, the Possessor, the Ruler who has legal power and authority. It is used not only of God but also of Christ.

(3). PATER- means Father in Greek. It expresses The relationship in which Christ as the Son Stands to God the Father. It further encompasses the relationship in which all Christian believers stand in Christ.

B) Attributes of God

The Attributes of God are divided into two categories: The Incommunicable and the Communicable Attributes.

(1). Incommunicable Attributes--These are personal to God alone and not transferable to man. They are:

(a) The self-existence of God; which means God has no origin. He is not a created being, but rather a self-sustained and self-generated Divine Spiritual Being. The angels and man are created beings; unlike God who is independent in Himself and on Him all of creation depends. This self-existence manifests itself in the name Jehovah.

(b). The Infinity of God is another aspect of His Incommunicable Attributes. He has no beginning and no end. God is not limited by time and space nor confined to the universe. He is both immanent and transcendent over His creation. By virtue of God's infinity, He is also (i) Absolute Perfection. God is eternally ageless and lives forever. Man's days are few and numbered, in contrast. (ii) His Immensity means that in relation to space, God's infinity occupies the entire universe as well as the whole of the heaven. The song says: " So high we cannot get over Him; so low we cannot get under Him; and so wide, we cannot get around Him." This means God transcends all "spatial limitations" and yet is present in every part of space with His whole Divine Being." (Ibid, p. 60)

From this vantage, God controls and regulates His creation. God is not absent from any part of the heaven and earth, nor more present in any one of them. He is immanent, so to speak. Still, He is not a part of the universe or what some call nature. Berkhof further states that God does not dwell on earth as He does in heaven; in animals as He does in man; in the inorganic as He does in the organic creation; in the wicked as He does in the pious nor in the Church as He does in Christ. (Ibid, p. 61) God's ability to be presents everywhere at the same time is called Omnipresence.

(c). The Immutability of God-- This Incommunicable Attribute pertains to Gods unchangeability, not immovability. In stead, in His Being and perfection as well as in His purposes and promises, God is constant. His foreknowledge, wisdom, sovereign power and will account for this Immutable character.

(d). The Unity of God. —This implies that there is but one Divine Being. Deut. 6:4 confirms this unity: "Hear O Israel; Jehovah our God is one Jehovah." God is simple and indivisible. By implication it is asserted that the three persons in the "Godhead are not so many parts of which the Divine essence is composed, that God's essence and perfections are not distinct, and that the attributes are not superadded to His essence." (Ibid, P62)

(2). The Communicable Attributes -- These are attributes of God that can also be found in man, but to a limited degree. (i) The spirituality of God. John 4:24 quotes Christ as saying "God is Spirit." Not simply spirit like the created spiritual beings. He is the Prime Spirit in all the essence of Spirit. This spirituality of God emphasizes the distinction of His Being from both the material and spirit world. By asserting God's spirituality we are saying that the finite mind cannot understand the entirety of His Being. He is therefore immortal, boundless and transcendent over creation. (ii) Intellectual Attributes. Here God is perfect in His intellectual attributes and all knowing, and all wisdom.

(a). The Knowledge of God enables Him to be the ultimate perfection. He alone knows Himself. The nature of this knowledge causes God to know the universe, as it exists in His own eternal idea prior to its existence as a finite reality in time and space. This absolute knowledge is unlike man's, which is derived from learning facts and ideas through observation of the Universe. God's knowledge is immediate and innate; not derived from observation or reasoning. It is simultaneous and not successive. Unlike God, man knows in part, and must constantly adjust his knowledge to new revelations as God progressively reveals them or as new evidence is made available. Thus, God's knowledge is said to be extent; all-inclusive. Therefore, "God is Omniscience; knowing Himself and in Himself all things that come from Him." (Ibid, pp. 66-67). In short, nothing is hidden from His eyes.

(b). The Wisdom of God-- This is knowledge based on the intuitive insight of things originating only in the essence of His Diving Being. Wisdom, like knowledge, is also imperfect in man. In God, the attributes are absolute and perfect in every respect. Consequently, God choices the means that produces the best result in every situation. He has the ability to direct the course of events both in heaven and on earth to bring glory to Himself.

(i). The Veracity of God—By this we mean God is faithful. He is a covenant keeping God. Jesus declared: "I am the truth." Hence He is perfectly reliable in His revelation that is why the Scripture is a reliable basis of our knowledge and faith in

God. He cannot lie. (See Ex. 34:6).

(iv). Moral Attributes—The moral attributes of God are His goodness, holiness and righteousness. These are further subdivided to indicate that God is loving; gracious; merciful and longsuffering (patient, not swift to anger and judgment). The foregoing attributes relate to His goodness. As to His Holiness, God is sinless and undefiled. He therefore abhors sin. He is holy in his goodness and grace as well as in His justice and mercy. Concerning the Righteousness of God, He strictly upholds His decrees (edits, designs and plans) and calls on heaven and earth to conform to them. His wrath is reserved for those who refuse to avail the means of grace He has provided in Jesus.

Decrees of God

The Decrees of God reveal his Sovereign eternal will for man and the entire universe, and are immutable—meaning they do not change. Example: We are told not to worship other gods or idols, but God Almighty. However, man in exercise of his free will does create false gods and worship them, contrary to Gods Sovereign will. Even if Idolatry is permitted under the laws of a country, God will still pass Judgment against the offender for violating his declared will. So, the exercise of free will does not abrogate the predetermined counsel of God. Only the blood of Jesus Christ can remove a person from the consequences of God's Righteous Judgment against sin.

C) The Holy Trinity

The Christian doctrine of the Trinity is grounded in the Holy Bible. The word Trinity is actually a term of art. It implies that God exist and manifests Himself in three co-equal Divine persons. The word trinity does not explicitly appear in the Holy Bible, but the idea is implied in both the Old and New Testaments. It was at the Council of Nicea (325 A.D.) that the early Pre-Reformation Church leaders coined the word and adopted the Nicean Creed to harmonize conflicting philosophical and Theological teachings about the Deity of Christ in Relation to God the Father, and God the Holy Spirit. Some had argued that Christ was a mere man (another prophet). The Hebrew word El ELOHIM connotes plural. Yet this plurality is one of Unity, referring to the one true God of the Jews.

Also, at the Council of Constantinople (281 A.D), the Deity of the Holy Spirit was in dispute. This Council did not precisely define the Deity of the Spirit as the Council of Nicea clarified that the Father, Son and Holy Spirit are of one substance and are worshipped and glorified as one Tri-Une God.

During the Post-Reformation ear, the Church had to contend with divergent views on the issue of the Trinity. The Arminians, Epiuscopius, Curcellaeus and Limborgh revived the argument of subordination. These groups respectively assigned to the Father certain preeminence over the other persons, in order of dignity and power. For example, Hegel spook of the " ...Father as God in Himself, of the Son as God objectifying Himself and of the Holy Spirit as God returning unto Himself. " (Ibid, p. 83). Schleiermacher, for his part, noted that the three persons in the Godhead are simply "three aspects of God." He concluded that the Father is God underlying unity of all things; the Son, as God coming to conscious personality in man; the Spirit as God living in the Church (Ibid). The Unitarians also added their voice to the debate, stating that Christ is a divine teacher, and identified the Holy Spirit with God the immanent Being.

Today, when Christians speak of the Trinity, they are declaring that there is a Trinity in Unity. A unity that is trinal. Compared with man, who is uni-personal, God is tri-personal. His tri-personality is the essential necessity in the Divine Being. Paul in Eph. 3:19 and Col. 1:19; 2:9 speaks of this pleroma (fullness) of the Godhead residing in Christ bodily. As in the Old Testament Jehovah is represented as the redeemer and savior of Israel, so does God the Son in the New Testament clearly stand out in that capacity revealing God in human bodily form. This is why Christ is called the God-man.

For His part, God the Holy Spirit dwells in the Church regenerating believers unto good works as well as guiding, teaching and comforting them. The confirmation of the Trinity also took place at the baptism of Christ when the heavens opened and the Spirit descended like a dove on Jesus, while God the Father declared from His eternal throne: "This is my beloved Son in whom I am well pleased (See Matt. 3:16, 17). Jesus Himself also commanded His disciples to baptize in the name of the Father, Son, and Holy Spirit." (See Matt. 28: 19).

Consequently, we can say without a doubt that the whole undivided essence of God belongs equally to each of the three persons in the Godhead. Yet, each person in the God-head is separate and distinct in personality as well as function. "In personal substance the Father is first; the Son second and the Holy Spirit third." (Ibid-P. 88). This order should not be construed to denote priority in origin and existence. The father is self-generated; the Son is begotten of the Father—not created—and the Holy Spirit proceedeth from both the Father and the Son.

D) The works of GOD

God the Father is prominently in the works of Creation, as well as in the generation of the Messiah-sonship, whose death on the cross completed the redemption of the world. Thus, all things begotten as well as those created, have their origin in the eternal Father (God) and flow through the Son who is the mediating cause of all creation.

Under God's plan of Redemption, the Holy Spirit planted the Son (Jesus) in Mary's womb to effectuate the eternal plan of salvation. The Son revealed God in the flesh. The Son also dwelled among the people of Israel pointing that representative group of mankind to the eternal love of the Father, His Decrees and His retributive Justice. The Son, Jesus Christ died on the cross and fulfilled the punishment reserved by God for mankind that resulted from Adam's disobedience. The eternal death and separation that fallen mankind is condemned to receive after physical death is no longer imposed on those who believe and accept the redemptive work of God the Son. The resurrection of Jesus therefore confirms His power over death and further assures mankind of their bodily resurrection just as Christ did. While Christ is absent from us bodily, the Holy Spirit continues to execute the divine work of regenerating believers unto worship of God and service to mankind. He enables believers to live a life of faith and to resist the entrapments of the devil. The Spirit dwells in the Church and directs its activities.

E) Gap Theory

The Bible says God created the universe in six literal days. The Hebrew word yom, which means day, as used in Genesis and other Books of the Pentateuch, conveys the idea of a 24 hour day comprising of both light and darkness.

However, in 1814, Thomas Chaulmers (1780 – 1847), a Scottish Theologian came up with a Gap Theory based on his interpretation of Genesis 1:1 and l: 2. He contended that there is a Gap between these two passages of Scripture, a lapse of 4 billion years between the creation of the heaven and the earth, and the creation of man, animals and Plants. The Gap Theory is also referred to as Ruin-and- Reconstruction Theory or Pre-Adamic Cataclysm Theory or the Restitution Theory or Progressive Creation Theory.

However, all of such teaching supports Evolution, and it is not Biblical at all. Still, Some Pastors and Evangelist are teaching Gap and Restoration Theology on Television. Following in Chaulmer's footsteps were Dutchman Episcopius (1583-1643), And Rev. William Buckland, a geologist, who gave the idea much undeserved publicity. Most notable among the 19th and 20th centuries' Gap theorists and writers are G.H. Pember, author of Earth's Earliest Ages, and Arthur C. Custance author of Without Form and Void, respectively. There are many Variations of The Gap Theory today, and you are now be equipt to identify them as Evolution Theory in disguise. Some folks just don't know what they are really preaching.

Generally, the explanation given in support of said "Gap" is that after God created heaven and earth, He created spirit beings (Angels), including Lucifer (Satan). Then Satan rebelled against God and was cast down, along with his hosts of demons, from heaven onto the earth. (See Ezekiel 28:13-15) A cataclysmic battle is said to have subsequently ensued between God and Satan, which destroyed the earth and it"became" without form, "void" and in a state of total darkness. Consequently, God recreated the earth, placed Adam and Eve in the Garden of Eden and commanded them to be fruitful multiply, "replenish," and subdue the earth (Genesis 1: 28).

Gap Theory further holds that in order for God to use the word "replenish" (Hebrew "male" or "mah-lay"), the earth must have been previously populated either before the six day creation mentioned in Genesis 1: 31 or before the earth became without form, void and dark, as recorded in Genesis 1:2.

All About God Ministries beautifully disproves the aforementioned tenets of Gap Theorists: "The word replenish has changed in meaning since the King James Version of the Bible was written in 1611 AD. At that time, the Hebrew word "male" [mah-lay] was used for the word "replenish," and it meant "to fill," as in an initial act of completion. The word "replenish" didn't take the meaning of "refilling" until it was incorporated into the English language about 1650 AD. The Hebrew word for "replenish," as in "refilling that which was once filled" is "shana." Genesis 1:28 uses the word "male" in the original Hebrew text. So, God told Adam to "go fill the earth," and did not imply a refilling or replenishing of what had once been filled or completed …" (See Gap Theory—No Support, Article published on AllaboutGod.Com).

Gap Theory and its problems

1. Gap Theory attempts to discredit the Bible and in doing so, it lends support to atheistic evolution which holds that the earth, man, animal and plants evolved over a period of about 4 billion years. According to the Theory, this accounts for The fossils found in various layers of the earth, by Geologist. However, carbon dating has not been able to conclusively substantiate these assertions. On the other hand, Christian scientists who believe in the Genesis 1: 1-2 literal six day creation, say the earth is about 6000 years old, and submit that it does not take billion of years for human, animal and plant remains to fossilize.

1. Some circular geologist also reject the gap theory, its geologic ages and geological column, as being invalid.
2. The Bible does talk about the earth being destroyed by flood during the days of Noah--Genesis 7 & 8. This is said to account for some of the rock and soil forms being misunderstood by Gap Theory.
3. Human and animal fossils have been found by other geologists beneath various layers of the earth. These fossils, we are told, cannot be the basis for the Gap Theory. They rather support the Biblical record of the flood.

In conclusion, Gap Theory is false and misleading in its interpretation of Genesis 1:1-2. It attempts an incorrect distinction between the Hebrew verbs bara, which means to create, and asha, which means to make. It also errs in translating the Hebrew verb hayetha, as became, when it means was. As such, proponents of the Gap Theory have twisted the

Biblical statement: "the earth was without form and was void ..." to read, "the earth became without form and void."

The Hebrew expression tohu wabohu, literally means "empty (void) and formless." It is therefore wrong to construe tohu wabohu (empty) as a state of disrepair, and use such translation to justify the assertion that the earth had to be recreated.

The prevailing Theological view is that the universe and all it contains were created by God in a literal six-day (Heb. yom) period; given shape and populated by God. Scripture does not support the view that Lucifer and his demons inhabited the Garden of Eden before Adam and Eve. The Gap Theory is therefore baseless and has no authoritative merit, and the Holy Scripture should be taken by faith as inerrant, infallible, divinely revealed and inspired by God.

F) Covenant Theology

Covenant Theologians say their doctrine is Biblical. A covenant is a legal word. It simply means agreement. It is an agreement usually made between two or more people for a clearly defined objective. It requires strict compliance with its terms and conditions. If one party to the covenant fails to perform as provided under the covenant, he is said to be in breach, and the penalty for noncompliance may be imposed.

Covenants are either unilateral or bilateral. A unilateral covenant or contract or agreement is one imposed by a higher authority, or the person who wants a given act to be performed. He is the offeror. The person or people to whom the offer is addressed (offerees), simply have to perform the conditions imposed. Performance of the act required amounts to acceptance of the covenant/agreement. For example, my dog gets missing and I place an Advertisement in a popular news paper offering to pay anyone who finds the dog $50.00. If you read my publication and find the dog, and deliver it to me, you have performed the contract, and are therefore entitled to the money. No formal ascceptance was necessary, only performance.

On the other hand, a bilateral covenant is a product of bargain between two or more people, from a presumed position of strength. There is mutuality of accent by the contracting parties. Such bilateral covenants require acceptance by the person to whom the offer is made, in order to be legally effective. Failure to accept the terms and conditions of the offer as submitted by the offeror, is a rejection, and there is no contract. Both the Old Covenant and the New Covenant of the Holy Bible are unilateral covenants. That means, the terms of the covenants are imposed by God. In part, the former is said to be work oriented (performance), while the latter is based only on acceptance/believing in Jesus Christ as Lord and Savior.

Before the Reformation, the early Church used the doctrine of the covenant in five principal ways: (1) To stress the moral obligations of Christianity. (2) To show God's grace in including the gentiles in the Abrahamic blessings. (3) To deny that Israelites received the promises simply because they are physical descendants of Abraham. (4) To Demonstrate the unity between the Old and New Covenants in Scripture. According to R. Scott Clark, Associate Professor of Historical Systematic Theology at Westminster Theological Seminary in California, the above numbered purposes were developed by the early church because of the Pelagian and semi-Pelagin (late 300's to early 400's), controversies. Prior to that time, the church did not have a clearly defined doctrine on salvation (See A Brief History of Covenant Theology by R. S. Clark).

Theologians of the Medieval Period held the view that God will only pronounce people righteous if they are truly righteous, inside and out. According to them, this happens when sinners are "fused with grace" so that they become saints. Hence justification was a matter of cooperation with divine grace. They therefore regarded faith as obedience and doubt as the absence of faith. Proponents of this belief were the Franciscan Theologians William of Ockham (1285-1347) and Gabriel Biel (1420 – 95). They taught that God does not say what he says (i.e. you are just) because we humans are really just, but because we have met the terms of the covenant to cooperate with God.

This teaching became the Franciscans' Pactum Theology. Its central theme is summed up in these words: "to the one who does what he can, God will not deny grace." This teaching is commonly referred to as "God helps those who help themselves." Both Ockham and Biel further taught that God rewards sinners when they do their best, and overlooks their sins and treats them as though they had fulfilled the terms of the covenant: i.e. the law. As such, they deny the doctrine of original sin.

On the other hand was Augustine of Hippo, who held a contrary view on the subject of Covenant Theology and original sin. In his work, City of God, Augustine outlined the central elements of Covenant Theology. He divided the doctrine into the Covenant of Works and the Covenant of Grace. He is quoted as saying: "But even the infants not personally in their own life, but according to the common origin of the human race have all broken God's Covenant in that one (Adam) in whom all have sinned." Augustine further said, " …there are many things called God's covenant besides the Old and New Covenants." He went on to say that the first covenant that was made by the first man is just this: "in the day ye eat thereof, ye shall surely die." This statement is in reference to the tree of life, which God prohibited Adam from eating.

Martian Luther, father of the Protestant Reformation, also expressed his views about Covenant Theology, but he did not out rightly abandon the Franciscans' Partum Theology. However, as he became a Protestant, Luther adhered to Paul's teaching on original sin and God's absolute sovereignty in salvation. He agreed with Paul and taught that the imputation of man's sin to Christ and his righteousness to us and faith in the work accomplished by Christ, as the only instrument of justification. Luther is quoted by Scott as saying: "we are not justified because we are sanctified." In short, Luther did not reject the idea of merit, but rather maintained that it is not of merits of any human being, produced by grace which pleases God; rather it is Christ who merited the justice of God in place of man, that what Christ merited is imputed to sinners.

Some scholars contend that John Calvin did not teach the same covenant theology latter Reformed Theologians had taught; because he did not use the same vocabulary. Ironically, it is indicated that Calvin had complained about the Romanists not allowing him to use the phrase "faith alone" (Institutes, 3.11.19), since the word "alone" (sola) is not expressly found in Scripture. It must, however, be noted that Calvin taught that the

Law (Covenant of works) kills sinners and the Gospel (Covenant of grace) justifies and sanctifies them through faith alone, in Christ. (Ibid, P. 8)

During the Reformation of the sixteenth century, Zwingli and Heinrich Bullinger also taught Covenant Theology in response to the Anabaptists in and around Zurich. Bullinger is said to have published the first treatise devoted to explaining the covenant in 1531. Like Calvin and the early fathers he used the covenant to teach the unity of God and his salvation. He is credited with using the covenant of grace as a summary of Biblical Theology. Caspar Olevin (1536-1587) further expanded on the teachings of the covenants in three works, chiefly in his book: On the Substance of the Covenant of Grace Between God and the Elect.

One of the lesser known Protestant Covenant Theologian was Johannes Oecolampadius (1531). His teachings on the subject of Covenant Theology are regarded as more remarkable and mature. In his teachings, he included the Covenant of Redemption, the Covenant of Works and the Covenant of Grace. Oecolampadius is considered by some to be the first Reformed Covenant Theologian. He taught that the Covenant of Redemption was made among God the Father, Son and Holy Ghost; maintaining that the Covenant of Grace is the out working of the Covenant of Redemption (Ibid, P. 10). Thus, Reformed Theology of the 17th century taught that the Father required the Son to obey in place of the elect, that He should be their surety; i.e. He would meet the legal obligations of the elect, to atone for their sins, to bear the punishment of their sins and to meet the demands of the covenant of works (Law) and to merit the forgiveness of sins and positively impute His righteousness to His people. In the 20th century, Urisinus opined that the covenant of works stands for the Law, which is not gracious, but relentless in its demand for perfection. The covenant of grace, he said, stands for the Gospel, which means that Christ, our Mediator and substitute, has met the terms of the law for us. According to him, the Covenant of Grace was a Covenant of Works for Christ. Therefore, it is Christ who produced the Gospel Covenant for us because of his obedience of the Father unto death. Urisinus further contends that unlike the Covenant of Works made with sinless Adam, the Covenant of Grace is made with sinners, who need a mediator, a Covenant keeping Savior, who fulfilled the law, satisfied God's just wrath for sinners. He said this is the difference between Law and Gospel. (Larger Catechism, Q, 36, quoted by Clark in His History of Covenant Theology).

The Covenant of Works or the Old Covenant

The Covenant of Works primarily refers to God's unilateral covenant with Adam in the Garden of Eden. Adam was specifically commanded by

God not to eat of the Tree of Life; if he did, he would surely die (Genesis 2: 15-17). The performance of this covenant provision was all God asked of Adam to guarantee his continual existence. He did not obey, but rather ate the forbidden fruit and was consequently expelled from the Garden of Eden. The Edenic covenant required absolute obedience, and that was work in itself. Adam's disobedience, commonly called the Fall of Man, brought sin and death into the world, so that every human being, young or old, rich or poor is condemn to die; eternally separated from God in hell.

There are Covenant Theologians who hold the view that another aspect of the Covenant of Works involves God's giving of the Law to Moses on Mount Siani. Israel had been brought out of slavery in Egypt and was commanded in the Ten Commandments to worship only God, keep the Sabbath; don't kill nor covet their neighbors' properties, and wives, among other things. Strict compliance with all of the laws contained in the Commandments was required and expected from Israel.

Considering the Adamic nature already passed on to all descendents of Adam, Israel could not and did not keep the laws of God. They were punished several times for their disobedience, including dispossession of the Promised Land. Animal sacrifices were made under the Old Covenant/Covenant of Works to atone for sins. These were not adequate because they were only effective for a short period of time, and sacrifice upon sacrifice had to be made constantly in order for God to forgive the sins of Israel.

Therefore, in His sovereign wisdom, love and concern for fallen man, God the Father, Son, and Holy Spirit devised a plan of Redemption, in order to save man from sin, and bring him into eternal fellowship with God; thereby abrogating or nullifying the Old Covenant/Covenant of

Works. (See Stephen Geard essay on Covenant Theology- Part 1, pp 1-3).

The Covenant of Redemption & the Covenant of Grace

Some modern day Covenant Theologians say there is a separate Covenant of Redemption, negotiated and entered into by and among the three Persons of the God Head, for the salvation or redemption of humankind. Others refer to it as a Plan of Redemption, making it the ultimate purpose of the Covenant of Grace. Grace being the means by which Redemption is obtained.

Consequently, we will discuss the Covenant of Grace as the primary and essential ingredient of God's Plan of Redemption or Salvation. Unlike the earlier covenant of works, whose mandate was "Do this and you shall live" (Rom. 10:5; Gal. 3:12), the Covenant of Grace is bestowed on humankind in their sinful condition with the promise that, inspite of our inability to keep any of the commandments of God, out of sheer grace God forgives our sins and accepts us as His children through the merits of His Son, the Lord Jesus Christ, on the condition of Faith. (Ibid, p. 1)

Under this New Covenant or Covenant of Grace, God the Father took upon Himself flesh and was born of the Virgin Mary; through the incarnation of the Holy Spirit. This means Jesus Christ is not the product of sexual intercourse between Joseph and Mary. As such, Christ did not inherit the Adamic nature, like every other person who is born of a woman. Christ became the God-man for the purpose of satisfying the demands of the Old Covenant, which was based on perfect works, and Justice (death) for noncompliance. In Heb. 7:22 Jesus is called the surety or guarantor of the new covenant, which is better than that which came through Moses. For Christ will bestow on all who believe in His death on the cross as a perfect and final ransom for sins, the blessings of eternal life. This belief, simply called faith in the Scripture, is the sole condition of the Covenant of Grace by which we are justified in Christ. The Covenant of Grace therefore abrogates and replaces the Old Testament Covenant of Works. So, According to Covenant Theologians, Israel, as a nation, has been replaced by the Church. That all of the Old Testament promises made to Abraham about the Land as well as the Davidic Messianic Kingdom of Christ has already been fulfilled. They hold that the Church now rules in the present world as the Kingdom of Christ among the unbelievers.

Current Opposition to Covenant Theology

1. In his essay: Covenant Theology Under Attack, Meredith G. Kline states that Daniel P. Fuller opposes the teachings of Reformed Covenant Theologians. Fuller is branded by him as not acknowledging a contrast between the covenant of works and the covenant of grace. He believes that grace was also present in the covenant of works; asserting that God did not have to create Adam, but He did so only because of grace. Therefore, grace is a part of the covenant of works.

2. Also, the Dutch-American Theologian, Herman Hocksema wrote: " ...it is quite impossible that man should merit a special reward with God. Obedience to God is an obligation ... Hence, we cannot accept the theory of the covenant of works, but must reject it as unscriptural."

3. Likewise, the Dutch-South African writer Cornelius van der Waal, is quoted by Geard as saying: "It is very clear

what was thought of as the nature of the so called covenant of works. Obedience to it would bring about righteousness through works. This notion must be radically rejected."

4. Professor Tom Wilkinson from Melbourne who lectured for many years at Reformed Theological College in Geelong, is quoted by Geard as saying the following: " ... to the covenant of works, there is the obligation that God's grace is swallowed up, giving the impression that it was to be a purely human achievement. Furthermore, whenever God's covenant is mentioned in the Bible, it has strong redemptive overtones which are absent from the concept of works. For these reasons there is doubt about the wisdom of speaking of a covenant of works (See Geard, Covenant Theology- Part 1, p. 5). According to Mal Couch, (author of An Introduction to Classical Evangelical Hermeneutics), Covenant Theologians believe in limited inerrancy of the Holy Scripture. As such, they engage in spiritualization and allegorization in their interpretation of Scripture. This "allows the exegete to manipulate the text to support his or her presuppositions" He further asserts: " ...When it comes to non-eschatological (Non End Time) literature, covenant theologians usually begin with a literal, grammatical-historical method of interpretation, referred to ... as a normal reading of Scripture. There are exceptions, however, especially when it comes to Israel and the Church. Often in Covenant Theology, Israel does not mean Israel; it is spiritualized to mean the Church. Regarding prophetic literature, the hermeneutics of Covenant Theologians are even more inconsistent, in that they consistently mingle an allegorical or spiritual method of biblical interpretation, with a normal reading of Scripture." (Mal Couch, p. 33).

Because of these inconsistent and subjective methods that Covenant Theologians are said to employ in their interpretation of Scripture, they fail to make a distinction between Israel as a nation and the Church. They hold the view that by virtue of the New Covenant mediated through the death of Jesus Christ, the Church has replaced the nation and people of Israel. Therefore they ignore the fact that God will in deed fulfill the unfulfilled portions of the Abrahamic Covenant regarding the land of Canaan that he gave to Israel forever, as an inheritance; the nation of Israel being the physical descendants of Abraham, Isaac and Jacob. Covenant Theologians also do not believe that Christ will fulfill the Davidic Covenant, which relates to the Messianic Kingdom. God had promised David an everlasting throne, on which Christ will sit and rule over Israel on earth during the Millennium Kingdom. However, Covenant Theology holds that by their rejection of Christ as their Messiah, the people of Israel also forfeited the Messianic Kingdom. Consequently, the Body of Christ, the Church, currently rules over the Messianic Kingdom of Christ. The Church comprises of both Jews and Gentiles who believe in Christ as their Lord and personal Savior. It is true that we Christian now live in the Kingdom of Jesus, even among the rest of the world. However, it is not the promised Millennium Kingdom, because the Church will not be here on earth when the Millennium Kingdom is established after the Great Tribulation. The Church would be seated in Heaven above after the rapture.

G) Dispensation Theology

The Greek word oikonomia, which means management of a house or economy, is the source of the English word Dispensation. It is a method or scheme according to which God carries out his purposes towards mankind. It is sometimes referred to as "the system by which things are administered" and "the divine administration or conduct of the world.

Theologically, it is a "religious order or system conceived as divinely instituted, or as a stage in a progressive revelation expressly adapted to the needs of a particular nation or period of time." " The English word economy, in its theological usage refers to the method of the divine government of the world or of a specific department or portion of that government."(See Dr. Renald E., Showers' essay, An Introduction to Dispensational Theology, p. 2). In summary, Dispensation Theology is defined as a system of theology that is primarily based on the Bible's philosophy of history as it relates to the rule or Sovereignty of God in the universe, and his plans of salvation for Israel and the Church, as two separate and distinct entities who he intends to reconcile and make one people of God, through Christ. Some Dispensationalist believe and teach that the Church will be a part of Jesus' Kingdom on earth, while others contend that the Church will be seated in heaven when Christ returns to establish his earthly kingdom and rule the world from Israel.

Before Clement of Alexandria (150-220 A.D.) and Augustine of Hippo (354-430 A.D.) the Church had no systematized teachings on Dispensation Theology. Alexandria is believed to have recognized and taught four dispensations of God's rule; while Augustine opined that God has employed several distinct ways of working in the world as He implements His divine plan for human history. It is however conceded that these two early Church leaders did not organize their teachings on the subject into a doctrine.

The French philosopher, Pierre Poiret (1646-1719) is credited as the first person to develop an authentic dispensational scheme in a systematic manner. His work on Dispensation is called The Divine Economy: A Universal System of the Works and Purposes of God Towards Men Demonstrated. Published 1687 in Holland. In His book, Poiret laid out seven dispensations that cover the scope of Scripture and history.

(Ibid, p. 1). Later in 1699, John Edwards is said to have published another well-developed dispensational scheme in his book: A Complete History or Survey of All the Dispensations. The Christian theologian and hymn writer, Isaac Watts also presented a system of six dispensations in his essay called The Harmony of all the Religions, which God ever prescribed to Men and all his Dispensations towards them. The subject of Dispensation Theology found its way into the 19th century, with John Nelson Darby of the Plymouth Brethren playing an important role in this debate. Dr. Showers credits him with developing, systematizing and spreading Dispensation Theology. Also, C.I. Scofield, producer of the Scofield Reference Bible made contribution to the study of dispensation theology. These are just a few Theologians who studied and wrote on the subject.

According to Dr. Showers, there are five important points to consider In the doctrine of Dispensation Theology. They are:

(1)" …The different dispensations are diffferent ways of God administering His rule over the world. They are not different ways of salvation. Through out history God has employed several dispensations, but only one way of salvation. Salvation has always been by the grace of God through faith in God. Today, this same God has based salvation through faith in the death of Jesus Christ.

(2) " …a dispensation is not an age of history, even though a dispensation may cover the same time period as an age. A dispensation is a particular way of God administering His rule, but an age is a particular period of time.

(3) " …a dispensation may involve a particular way of God administering His rule over all of mankind or over only one segment of mankind. For example, the Dispensation of Human Government was over all of mankind, but the Dispensation of the Mosaic Law was over only the nation of Israel.

(4) " …a new dispensation may continue or discontinue some
ruling factors of previous dispensations, but it will have at least
one new ruling factor never introduced before. Dispensation
Theologians normally name each new dispensation after the new
ruling factor or factors. " …each new dispensation demands new
revelation. God must reveal His new way of ruling and man's
new responsibility near the beginning of each dispensation.
Dispensation Theology recognizes several successive dispensations,
but has a strong concept of progressive revelation." (Ibid., p. 3)

For his part, Mal Couch, says dispensationalists basically agree on
seven (7) dispensations. They are:

1. Dispensation of innocence
2. Dispensation of conscience
3. Dispensation of government
4. Dispensation of promise
5. Dispensation of Law
6. Dispensation of the church (or grace)
7. Dispensation of the kingdom (1000 years rule of Christ
   after the rapture).

(See Mal Couch, An Introduction to Classical Evangelical Hermeneutics,
A Guide to the History and Practice of Biblical Interpretation Kregel
Publication, 2000, p. 171)

Literal Interpretation of Scripture

Based on the above, Dispensation Theologians contend that scripture
must be literally interpreted. They therefore analyze the words of scripture,
the context in which they are used, the grammar employed, and study
the historical and cultural setting of each genre to arrive at an accurate

interpretation of the meaning the Biblical author intends to convey, as well as how the people to whom those words were addressed, understood them. Consequently, Dispensationalists reject spiritualization of the content of Scripture in its totality. According to them, the Old Testament should not be read into the New Testament, and verse versa. Strange, right? Is the Old not the shadow of the New, and is the New not the fulfillment of the Old? I believe they complement each other, and that is how God intended them to be.

Israel and the Church are different

Because they believe that the Old Testament and the New Testaments should be handled Differently, Dispensation Theologians believe that the Church is separate and distinct from Israel. This means, the promise of the land and the messianic kingdom promised Abraham and his descendants, Israel, in Scripture, do not belong to the Church. However, the Church is by scripture destined to participate in that aspect of Abraham's promise, which relates to the rest of mankind being blessed through the seed of Abraham. That seed is Christ, whose sacrificial death on the cross reconciled both Jews and gentiles into one united sonship in God through Jesus Christ. By His death, Christ mediated a better covenant, which for all intents and purposes abrogates, repeals, and replaces the Leviticus priesthood and the law.

Why? Because the Old Testament priesthood and the animal sacrifices they offered day after day and year after year, were not perfect and sufficient to atone for the sins of the people of Israel, It became necessary for God to offer up Christ as the one final sacrifice for the atonement of the sins of the whole world. So, all gentiles as well as Jews who believe in Christ, now receive eternal salvation through Christ, the new high priest who lives in heaven, eternally interceding before God on their behalf. (Ibid p.173-175)

For Biblical support, see Hebrews 7:11, 12, 19 & 22 states:

"If therefore perfection were by the Leviticus Priesthood, (for under it the people received the law,) what further need was there that another Priest should rise after the Order of Melchizedek, and not be called after the order of Aaron?

"For the priesthood being changed, there is made of necessity a change also of the law ...

"For the law made nothing perfect, but the bringing of a better

Hope did; by which we draw nigh unto God ...

"By so much was Jesus made a surety of a better testament."

Yet, this does not mean that the Church now stands in the place of Israel. Israel is still the physical seed of Abraham. The Jews are entitled to their promised land in Canaan and the future kingdom with Christ as their messianic king. The adopted gentiles (the church), who become sons of God through Christ, as well as Jews who receive Christ as their savior will become the beneficiaries of eternal life in heaven, during the entire duration of the millennial kingdom. Dispensationalists therefore believe in the premillennium rapture of the Church before the tribulation. Amillennialists reject the Kingdom Postponement Theory, arguing that when Israel rejected Christ during his first coming; they also forfeited the promised Davidic Kingdom, arguing that the Church is the new Israel. Dispensationalists further insist that as a nation and people, the Jews will persist in their unbelief of Christ until the Church is raptured. Then Christ, the Deliverer and Messiah will return and restore the Jews to their land and ungodliness will be turned away from them, because he will remove their sins and write his laws upon their hearts and place his Spirit in them (as He does the Church on earth). Thus, the Church will not go through the tribulation. Israel and the rest of the gentile nations who do not believe in Christ will experience it. As Isaiah and other Old Testament prophetic books foretold the virgin birth of Christ, and those prophecies were fulfilled, so will the New Testament Teachings of His second coming be literally fulfilled, Dispensationalists assert.

The Gospel of Matthew is referred to as the Manifesto of Jesus' Kingdom message to Israel. In it He declares the essential character of the Messianic Kingdom, and lays down conditions of entrance into the kingdom. For example, when Jesus entered into Jerusalem He was proclaimed King of the Jews; at His trial before Pilate, He did not decline the title, King of the Jew. At the top of His cross, was written King of the Jews.

It goes, with out further argument that while on earth, the mission of Jesus was not to establish the church, but rather to prepare Israel for the Kingdom of God with Christ as its King. In fact, this is the central theme of Matthew's Gospel. Under the New Covenant between Christ and the Jewish nation, the kingdom Jew is given access to the land, and the Messianic Kingdom, via the Blood of Christ. Jeremiah 31:33, "I will make a new covenant with the house of Israel and the house of Judah … I will put My law in their inward parts, and write it upon their hearts." Such Jews, according to some Dispensation Theologians, will make up the Kingdom of Christ upon his second coming, to establish His millennium kingdom after the rapture of the Church.Dispensationalist who hold this view, also say that the Church was never intended to be a partaker of the blessings of the kingdom with Israel. Rather, the Church will inherit and dwell in heaven as the bride of Christ. It is further indicated that some dispensationalists, do not agree that there are two Gospels, each dependent upon the Blood of the Cross-- One is earthly, the other is heavenly. And both Gospel are "according to Jesus." While on earth, Christ in His humiliation, (prior the Cross) ministered the Gospel of the earthly Kingdom of Israel, under the New Covenant promised by Jeremiah. On the other hand, the mystery of the Church remained hidden, but it was subsequently revealed to Paul by the glorified Lord Jesus, after Calvary, from heaven, exclusively for His chosen heavenly people, His beloved Bride, the Church. The Church's inheritance is located in heaven, and she was manifested on the earth at Pentecost. As such, the Church had no relationship to anything prior to the Cross. (See Miles J. Stanford's essay, The Dispensational Gospels, p. 5)

Finally, Dispensation Theologians believe in the full inerrancy of the Holy Scripture, and therefore interpret Scripture literally. They allow no room for spiritualization or allegorization of Scripture. According to them, the Bible says what God means and means what he says; so Scripture must be interpretated objectively and consistently. Dispensationist contend that a clear distinction must be made between Israel and the Church. Israel, they say, was given unconditional promises in the Old Testament that will be fulfilled during the Millennium Kingdom of Christ. That God has merely suspended performance of those promises during this Church age of grace. Yet, the Abrahamic covenant concerning the promised land and the future messianic kingdom confirmed by God in the Davidic Covenant, will be fulfilled at Christ's second coming after the rapture of the Church. Therefore, the church is not the new Israel, but a new mystery not revealed in the Old Testament. They insist that through out history God has established and relied on a single way of salvation, not two ways of salvation as Covenant Theologians contend. Faith in God, Dispensationists submit, has always been the basis of salvation, and not works through the Leviticus priesthood or the Mosaic Law. That the sacrifices established in Leviticus were the means by which the people of Israel received forgiveness of sins, while the law was for governance of the nation of Israel. Irrespective of these, the people still had to believe in God and trust Him as their creator and sustainer, just as Abraham believed in God and was declared righteous on the basis of his faith alone. As such, no amount of works could purchase this righteousness or justification. Similarly, under the Dispensation of Grace, it is faith in Christ alone that assures our salvation. Justification and righteousness come only through faith in the substitutionary death of Christ. Both Jews and Gentiles who put their trust in Christ as Savior, are cleansed from their sins, reconciled and become part and parcel of the Body of Christ, the Church, a new entity that is separate and distinct from the Nation of Israel.

H) The Doctrine of Revelation

The doctrine of revelation holds that God has revealed Himself to man progressively in two main ways. (1) Through His works of creation, God reveals Himself as the creator of the universe and all that it contains, including man, the planets, plaints and animal lives. In Psalm 19:1-2 we read: " The heavens declare the glory of God; and the Firmament showeth his handiworks." This revelation of God as seen from all that exist in the universe is called General Revelation. Yet, God is not fully revealed in the universe, because by looking at the universe man does not get to understand the divine nature of God. Neither do we get to comprehend what needs to be done in order to be saved.

God also reveals Himself in the pages of the Holy Bible, as well as in the person of Jesus Christ. This is called specific revelation. The Scripture tells us what God's sovereign will concerning mankind is. The Scripture also tells us about the birth of Christ as the savior of the world, for the redemption of our sins. In the Bible we are also told about the life, works and subsequent death and resurrection of Jesus. We are assured of Christ's return to earth, and that by putting our faith in the substitutionary death of Christ; mankind can escape eternal death and separation from God. In a conversation with Thomas and Philip, Christ Himself declared in John 14:7-10, the following: "If ye had known me, ye should have known my Father also, and from henceforth ye know him, and have seen him. Philip saith unto him, Lord, show us the Father, and it sufficeth us. Jesus saith unto him, have I been so long time with you, and yet hast thou not known me, Philip? He that hath seen me hath seen the Father; and how sayest thou then, show us the father? Believest thou not that I am in the Father, and the Father in me? The words that I speak unto you I speak not of myself, but the Father that dwelleth in me, he doeth the works."

In John 1:18 we find: "No man hath seen God at any time; the only begotten Son, which is in the bosom of the Father, he hath declared him." Christ, therefore, is a picture of God the Father. Both through Christ and the Scripture, we learn about the love of God and all other attributes of His, discussed in this paper. Therefore, the Bible and Christ constitute a full revelation of God, and all that Scripture contains is sufficient to give us a better understanding of God, our creator.

Inspiration and Authority of Scripture

The Bible is divinely inspired by God, meaning that God Himself revealed and communicated to the human authors of the Bible the words that they wrote. As such, Scripture is said to be authoritative and accurate. It contains all that God wants us to know about Him, as well as what He expects of us. 2 Timothy 3:16-17 state: "All scripture is given by inspiration of God, and is profitable for doctrine, for reproof, for correction, for instruction in righteous. That the man of God may be perfect, thoroughly furnished unto all good works."

The purpose of revelation is to communicate knowledge to the writers of Scripture. While inspiration has to do with securing infallibility in teaching. Therefore the Precepts contained in the Bible, both Old and New Testaments are reliable. They are not the product of human philosophy and wisdom. Rather, the Bible is the unadulterated word of God Himself. It contains the whole counsel of God concerning all things necessary for his own glory, man's salvation, faith, and life. We are therefore enjoined by Scripture not to add to nor subtract from the word of God as written in the Bible, for there is no new revelation to be added. The Bible is the whole extant supernatural revelations of God designed to be a rule of faith and practice.

The Inerrancy of Scripture

(a)Inerrancy of the Scripture relates to its infallibility and accuracy as to the teachings revealed to its authors by God. It does not mean that the sacred writers of Scripture were free from errors in conduct, as human beings. But, as to matters of spiritual doctrines revealed and inspired by the Holy Spirit, the authors of the Bible are said to be correct in what they wrote in the Bible. Therefore, Scripture cannot contradict Scripture, but rather supplement, compliment and or explain other portions of the Bible.

There are some who contend that there are discrepancies in the Bible as to Historical data, time and places. It should however be noted that these discrepancies are trivial, and do not affect the substance of the precepts, teachings and information contained in the Bible. These errors are usually the product of transcription and translation.

Souvereignty of God

This communicable attribute is absolute in God. However, government established on earth to regulate the affairs of men are partakers of God's Sovereignty only in a representative capacity. God's sovereign attributes include His Sovereign Will (decretive and perceptive) and His Sovereign Power. In short, His will is forever settled in heaven and on earth (e.g. The 10 commandments). By His Sovereign Power, God enforces his will and decrees, thus we say God is Omnipotent. All-powerful EL SHADDAI (Ibid, pp. 76-81).

I) Traducianism

Since God created Adam from the dust and breathed into his nostrils the breath of life, thereby making Adam a living Soul (Genesis 2:7), does God also breath into every subsequent descendent of Adam the breath of life upon or after conception in order for him or her to receive a soul? Or, by virtue of God's command that Adam and Eve should be fruitful and multiply, the human soul is automatically transferred from parents to their children? There is no unanimous theological consensus on the origin of the human soul or spirit, after the creation of Adam's soul by God. There are two major theological schools of thought on this subject. One called the Traducianism and the other, Creationism. Mid way between these two views, is Generationism. Let us take a brief look at the origin of the human spirit, sometimes wrongly confused with the soul, and investigate the merits and demerits of the above contending positions.

The prefix, tradux, refers to the shoot or sprout, root or vine of a plant that is capable of reproducing or propagating the species. The suffix, cianism, stands for the person who believes or teaches a given doctrine. Therefore, theologically speaking, Traducianism is the belief that the human spirit/soul is transmitted to the offspring by his/her parents. The doctrine is said to be "materialistic" because it holds that the soul of a child is transmitted through the organic process of generation.

Proponents of Traducianism

Tertullian (declared a heretics) is considered the first Christian Theologian to espouse Traducianism. Then came Rufinus, Apollinarus, and Gregory of Nvssa. They were later followed in this doctrine by Martin Luther, father of the Protestant Reformation and founder of the Lutheran Church, and some Western as well as North African Christian Churches.

Scriptural basis for Traducianism

(1) God's breathing into man the breath of life is not said to be repeated after Adam. Genesis (2:7);

(2) Adam begot a son in his own likeness (Gen. 5:3);

(3) God's resting (Gen. 2:2 - 3) suggests no fresh acts of creation ex nihilo; and

(4) Original sin affects the whole man, including the soul; this is simply accounted for by traducianism" (See Article by J.S. Wright, Believe Information Web Site).

(5) That the creation of Eve's Soul was included in that of Adam since she is said to Be of the man (I Cor. 11:8), and nothing is said about the creation of her soul. Gen. 2:3.That descendents are said to be in the loins of their fathers. Gen. 46: 26; Heb. 7: 9, 10.

(6) It is supported by the analogy of vegetable and animal life, in which the increase in numbers is secured, not by a continually increasing number of immediate creations, but **by the natural derivation of new individuals from a parent or stock. Ps. 104:30.**

(7) It also seeks support in the inheritance of mental peculiarities and family traits, which are so often just as noticeable as physical resemblances, and which cannot be accounted for by education, since they are in evidence even when parents do not live to bring up their children..

(8) Finally, it seems to offer the best basis for the explanation of the inheritance of moral and spiritual depravity, which is a matter of the soul rather than of the body. It is quite common to combine with Traducianism the realistic theory to account for original sin."

(Berkhof, p. 198)

Objections to Traducianism

Berkhof has raised 5 objections to Traducianism: (1) He believes that it runs contrary to the philosophical doctrine of the simplicity and indivisibility of the soul. (2) Admitting that the soul is transmitted from parents to children would affirm the misconception that the soul had a prior existence (pre-existence); that the soul is potentially present in the sperm or egg cells of the man or woman or both—thereby leading to materialism while making the parents creators. (3) IF God only works mediately, since His creative work seized on the sixth day (as Tranducianism contends), then what becomes of the doctrine of regeneration, which is not affected by second causes. (4) Traducianism is bound to the theory of realism, because this would be the only reason it can give for original guilt. Accepting this position would support the numerical unity of the substance of all human soul, which is untenable. (5) Traducianism would make Christ a sinner because his human nature is derived from Adam (Ibid).

J) Creationism

According to Creationism, every time a child is born, God immediately creates and infuses into his material body a soul that is separate, independent and distinct from the souls of his or her parents. God creates the soul from no preexisting material. Creationism insists that if it can be accepted that the soul comes from the semen of the man or the eggs of the woman, the soul would also be corporeal and subject to corruption.

Some proponents of Creationism

Francis Turretin had this to say about Creationism: (1) that from the law of creation, the origin of every human soul has to be the same as the origin of Adam's Soul. Why, because the formation of Adam is the example of the

90

creation of all men just as his marriage to Eve is the example of matrimony between all men and women. Terretin notes that the soul of Adam was made immediately by God when he breathed into Adam the breath of life and Adam became a living soul. Because the soul of Adam was created from nothing, so also the souls of Adam's descendents are created out of nothing. As to the soul of Eve, he observes that even though Scripture does not specify that God breathed into her the breath of life to become a living soul, by deduction, it is logical to conclude that God created a separate soul for Eve. She did not inherit her soul from Adam, even though she was created from his rib. The origin of Eve's soul could in no way be different from the origin of Adam's soul. Had it been otherwise, Adam would have exclaimed, "this is bone of my bone and soul of my soul." He only said "bone of my bone." (Gen. 2:23).

Turretin also states that from Scripture we are told that God is the author and creator of the soul in a way that is different from the body. He quotes Eccl. 12:17: "Then shall the dust return to the earth as it was, and the spirit shall return unto God who gave it." Because the body returns to the dust it came from and the soul to God who gave it, this shows two separate origins and final destinations. (See Francis Turretin, Creationism or Traducianism?-Thirteen Questions: on the origin of the Soul, published on the web site of A Puritin's Mind).

Aristotle, Jerome, Pelagius, John Calvin, modern Roman Catholicism and some Reformed Theologians also support the view that the soul is created by God and placed in the body for every conception of a human being, while the material corruptible body is derived from the parents sperm and egg cells. The Genesis account of creation states that the body was taken from the earth, while the spirit came directly from God, they assert. According to Berkhof, "This distinction is kept up throughout the Bible, where body and soul are not only represented as different substances, but also as having different origins," (See Berkhof, p, 199). We also read in Isa. 42:5: "The Lord forms the spirit of man within him."

Objections to Creationism

The following objections are raised in Berkhof's book:

(1) If the notion that the soul has original depraved tendencies is allowed to stand, then Creationism would make God the direct cause for moral evil.

(2) On the other hand, If the soul is said to have been created by God in a pure and unperverted state, then God is indirectly responsible for moral evil because he placed a pure soul in a corrupted sinful and depraved materal body, that will contaminate the soul.

(3) It considers the human father of a child as the procreator of only the material body of his child. This does not answer how the father's mental and moral traits are transmitted to his offspring.

(4) Creationism teaches a direct and on going process of creation by God if it is accepted that He creates a new soul each time a child is conceived or born. This assertion is inconsistent with the doctrine of secondary causes, as a means by which God cooperates with his creatures presently, to effectuate His sovereign decrees. (Ibid, pp. 199-200).

Some Arguments in support of Creationism

Inspite of the above criticism of Crationism, Berkhof seems to prefer it because " …it does not encounter the insuperable philosophical difficulty with which Traducianism is burdened; it avoids the Christological errors which Traducianism involves; and it is most in harmony with our covenant idea. At the same time we are convinced that the creative activity of

God in originating human souls must be conceived as being most closely connected with the natural process in the generation of new individuals.

Creationism does not claim to be able to clear up all difficulties, but at the same time it serves as a warning against ... the errors that the soul is divisible; that all men are numerically of the same substance and that Christ assumed the same numerical nature which fell in Adam." (Ibid, p. 201).

Generationism

Midway between Traducianism and Creationism is Generationism. Some early Church Fathers hesitated between Generationism and Creationism. Generationism states that the soul of the offspring originates from the parental soul in some mysterious way analogous to that in which the organism's material body originates from its parents seeds. St. Augustine was the most prominent of the early Fathers who thought that Generationism, unlike Creationism, seems to give the only explanation of the transmission of original sin. For their part, Saint Victor and Alexander of Hales, saw Generationism merely as more probable, but not the only explanation for the origin of the soul and sin. In recent times Generationism has been rejected by most Catholic theologians in favor of Creationism. The few exceptions include Rosmini " who asserts that the sensitive soul is generated by the parents, and becomes spiritual when God illuminates it and manifests to it the idea of which is the foundation of the whole intellectual life." Secondary causes (See Article on Traducianism on New Advent Web Site.). In summary, let me submit to you that God dose create a new spirit for every individual that comes into this world. In Jeremiah 1:5 we find these words: "Before I formed thee in the belly I knew thee; and before thou camest forth out of the womb I sanctified thee, and I ordained thee a prophet unto the nations." Friend, you are special and unique in every respect.

L) Predestination and the Sovereignty of God

As it relates to eternal salvation and the condemnation of the human spirit after physical death, Predestination is a controversial Biblical and Theological Christian Doctrine. It could serve as a stumbling block to the proclamation of the Gospel of Redemption in Christ, if it is not properly understood and taught. In it, some might find an excuse not to respond to the grace of God in Christ, believing that God has already predetermined their final destination or fate, and therefore see no effect in accepting or rejecting Christ as the only source of eternal salvation.

Yet, Predestination should be perceived and understood as a product of God's communicable intellectual essence. He is all knowing, omniscience. He knows the beginning as well as the end of all things, and sees them in their totality as a consummated present and final act, not things of the future. Man, on the other hand, sees in part, and therefore lacks the ability to know all that God knows except through the progressive revelation by God of what He has already ordained and imposed in eternity past (that is, before the creation of both the universe and man). In His Sovereign Power, God has already decreed His Sovereign Will, and has the ability to fulfill it by whatever means He choices, with or without the use or intervention of human agencies. God is also good, righteous and holy, patient and full of grace, in His Moral Essence. A discussion of the doctrine of Predestination **must, therefore, be done with the foregoing premise in mind, as one** investigates the teachings of Augustine, Luther, Calvin and others.

Augustine (413-426 AD) on Predestination

According to Louis Berkhof, Predestination, in this age, concerns "the counsel of God concerning fallen men, including the sovereign election of some and the righteous reprobation of the rest." (See Louis Berkhof, Systematic Theology, New Edition, 1996 p.109). Called Double Predestination, Hippo's St. Augustine is given credit for being the first

Christian Theologian to have given this view classical shape. He contended that God chose from all eternity who all would come into the kingdom of God, to replace the fallen angels, and thereby fill up the ranks of the heavenly choir. Augustine maintained that since Adam's fall, all humankind was under the curse of original sin and could not hope to have life with God after death without God's saving action. He also understood that the substitutionary death of Christ on the Cross was God's choice to save elected sinners, and by doing that, God's mercy is shown. Augustine espoused the view that God also chose to allow others to remain in their sins, unsaved in order to show God's Justice. Those predestined to eternal life were entirely a decision of God's Sovereign Will and Power.

Only those God had chosen from all eternity could turn away from their sins to God, because God would grant them grace and the power through the Holy Spirit to accept the grace of God. In summary, Augustine recognized that God must first take the initiative to give grace to sinners so that they can turn to God. This caused a controversy in the middle ages and a church council was convened. There the Semi-Pelagins of France admitted that divine grace alone produces salvation. However, they "resisted the doctrine of predestination based on foreknowledge (Ibid, p. 110). This denial of foreknowledge that God already knows who would be saved must, to all intent and practical purposes, be seen as a rejection by the Semi-Pelagins, of the premise that God in His Omniscience attribute, knows those who will be eventually saved.

Martin Luther on Predestination

Luther, a follower in the footprints of Augustine, rigidly adhered to Augustine's teachings on Predestination. However, In later years, he adopted a moderate single position on Predestination, recognizing that divine election was the cause of our salvation and that the human doctrine of free will and of our spiritual powers are futile. According to Luther, salvation does not depend on our will but on God's will and election. Yet, he does not hold the view that atonement is limited to the elect and refused to teach irresistible grace. Nevertheless, Luther propagated Universal grace and man's power to resist and reject the Gospel. He opined:

"Since salvation is totally of God's doing, the doctrine of election comforts those who believe. We can say, I belong to God! God has chosen me. I am one of his sheep." (Brian G. Mallson, **Double or Nothing: Martin Luther's Doctrine of Predestination** (1997).

Thus, Luther taught that God in eternity past did indeed elect a people for himself whom he would actively save in the outworking of history. But that God did not decree that the rest of mankind would absolutely be lost and consign them to eternal hell. In his work, Bondage of the Will, Luther asserts that the will of man must cooperate with the will of God in the reception of the gospel. That man's will is however bound in sin and therefore is completely unable to cooperate with God. Consequently, the Sovereign grace of God must be the sole determination in the salvation of man (Ibid).

John Calvin on Predestination

Calvin, a French Reformed Theologian and founder of the Presbyterian Church, is an adherent to Augustine's Double Predestination. He taught that in eternity past, prior to creation of the universe, God chose and elected a people for Himself whom he would actively save in the outworking of history. That God decreed that some will be saved and others would be lost. He further indicated that by attributing foreknowledge to God, we mean that all things have ever been, and perpetually remain, before His eyes. According to such knowledge of God, nothing is in the future or past, but all things are present in a manner that He does not merely conceive of them from ideas formed in His mind, as things remembered by us appear present to the human minds. Rather, God beholds and sees things as if actually placed before Him. This foreknowledge extends to the entire world, and to all the creatures created by God. Hence, Calvin asserts that Predestination is the eternal Decree of God by which He has predetermined in Himself the destiny of all things created, including man. Calvin believes that eternal life is foreordained for some, and eternal damnation for others (Double Predestination). Out of this came TULIP, the five major points of Calvinism.

(1) Man is totally deprived as a sinner. Man is deaf, blind and dead to the things of God. His will is in bondage to his evil and therefore man cannot choose to do good and resist evil in the spiritual realm. (2) That God has already chosen certain individuals to be saved even before the foundation of the world, based on His own Sovereign Will. This choice is not the result of man's faith and repentance. It is the consequence of God's prior election of them to be saved. For this reason God gives them the ability to repent and be faithful to Him. (3) There is Limited Atonement, not Universal Atonement.Only those fore-elected unto salvation, the Spirit gives faith to believe and accept Christ's death as the means of their salvation from eternal damnation. (4) Irresistible Grace is given to the elect such that inspite of the general call to repentance for salvation, only the elect by the workings of the Holy Spirit are extended special inward grace that inevitably brings them to salvation. The elect cannot reject this call no matter how hard they try. (Paul Modern History Sourcebook: John Calvin on Predestination, (June 1998, pp 141-150).

From the foregoing, one can clearly see that Calvin's doctrine of election; limited atonement and irresistible grace are contingent on God's Sovereign Will, Sovereign Power, as well as His foreknowledge. From the foundation of the world and the creation of man, God in his perfect Knowledge and Wisdom knew that sin would enter into the world, and that there would be some who will refuse to accept God's remedy for sin, the substitutionary death of Christ. That those who accept Christ would be the once whom God already knows would be saved through the exercise of their free will. This does not mean that John 3:16 is inoperative. There is still a general call to salvation;but not everybody who hears the Gospel will come to the saving grace it offers and guarantees in Christ.

The ultimate consequence of their refusal to avail themselves of God's grace, is eternal damnation. This is consistent with God's Sovereign Decree against sin. Simply put, sin will be judged. Those who repent and accept Christ are for all practical purposes the elect according to God's eternal purpose in eternity past. To hold otherwise would be a misconstruction of Calvin.

Universalism

This doctrine was spearheaded by John Murrary (17-1815). It holds that every individual in due time will be separated from sin. Like him, Hasea Ballou (1771-1852) taught that all people are saved and that there is no eternal punishment. Universalist deny the Trinity, saying that God is one person, Jesus was created, and that the Holy Spirit is not a person. Some believe that outside Christ there can be salvation after death, through a process of purification in the presence of God. Punishment for sin is not eternal, some assert.

This teaching is not Biblical. Ephesians 2:11-17 states: "Wherefore remember, that ye being in time past Gentiles in the flesh, who are called Uncircumcision by that which is called Circumcision in the flesh made by hands; that at that time ye were without Christ, being aliens from the commonwealth of Israel, and strangers from the covenants of promise, having no hope, and without God in the world: But now in Christ Jesus ye who sometimes were far off are made nigh by the blood of Christ. For he is our peace who hath made both one, and hath broken down the middle wall of partition between us.

Having abolished in his flesh the enmity, even the law of commandments contained in ordinances; for to make in himself of twain one new man, so making peace; and that he might reconcile both unto God in one body by the cross, having slain the enmity thereby; and came and preached peace to you which were afar off, and to them that were nigh."

"For whom he did foreknow, he also did predestinate to be conformed to the image of his Son, that he might be the first-born among many brethren. Moreover whom he did predestinate, them he also called: and whom he called, them he also justified: and whom he justified, them he also glorified. What shall we then say to these things? If God be for us, who can be against us? He that spared not his own Son, but delivered him up for us all, how shall he not with him also freely give us all things. Who shall lay any thing to the charge of God's elect? It is God that justifieth" (Romans 8: 29-33).

Predestination is Biblical. It is the recognition of God's foreknowledge of everything that happens before it ever takes place. This includes the knowledge of all those who will accept Christ as their savior and be spared eternal condemnation, as well as those who will not make use of the opportunity provided by Christ for the entire world to be saved.

The confusion about Predestination is a result of misinterpreting Augustine, Luther and Calvin. All of these early Christian Theologians are in agreement on the subject. The words chosen to express their thoughts may not be the most appropriate. However, they are united on the most important point of justification by faith in Christ, through the regenerative power of the Holy Spirit, who provides grace to all who are fore-called unto salvation in keeping with God's eternal Sovereign will, that humanity should be saved.

This grace is resistible because of man's free will. Yet, those who accept Christ as their savior are given the power through the Spirit to yield to God's grace. Atonement can be regarded as limited because it is reserved for those who accept Christ. In this sense alone is it limited, since God already knows that everybody will not be saved, as much as he desires them to escape eternal damnation. The human will is in bondage because of the fallen state of man in Adam. However, the will is not inextricably bound since God has provided the means of salvation to everybody. The call to salvation is therefore universal.

Rejection of this call is an individual decision because man has a freedom to choose Christ or reject His offer of salvation. He who refuses this grace accepts the eternally decreed penalty of death, in vindication of God's Holiness and Righteousness.

Bible verses supporting predestination

1. Deuteronomy 7:6-8 "For thou art a holy people unto the Lord thy God, the Lord thy God hath chosen thee to be a special people unto himself, above all people that are upon the face of the earth. The Lord did not set his love upon you, nor choose you, because ye were more in number than any people; for ye were the fewest of all people. But because the Lord loved you, and because he would keep the oath which he had sworn unto your fathers, hath the Lord brought you out with a mighty hand and redeemed you out of the house of bondmen, from the land of Pharaoh king of Egypt."

2. Jeremiah 1:5 "Before I formed thee in the belly I knew thee; and before thou camest forth out of the womb I sanctified thee, and I ordained thee a prophet unto the nations."

3. Psalm 78:70 "He chose David also his servant, and took him from the sheepfolds."

4. John 6:70 "Have I not chosen you twelve, and one of you is a devil?"

5. Matthew 17:14 "For many are called, but few are chosen."

6. Romans 11:5 "Even so then at this present time also there is a remnant according to election of grace."

7. Romans 9:11-13 "For the children being not yet born, neither having done any good or evil, that the purpose of

God according to election might stand, not of works, but of him that calleth; It was said unto her, the elder shall serve the younger. As it is written, Jacob have I loved, but Esau have I hated."

8. Romans 8:29-30 "For whom he did foreknow he also did predestinate to be conformed to the image of this Son, that he might be the first-born among many brethren. Moreover whom he did predestinate, them he also called: and whom he called, them he also justified: and whom he justified, them he also glorified."

9. Romans 8:33 "Who shall lay any thing to the charge of God's elect? It is God that justifieth."

10. 2 Timothy 2:10 "Therefore I endure all things for the elect's sake, that they may also obtain the salvation which is in Christ Jesus with eternal glory."

11. 1 Thessalonians 1:4 "Knowing, brethren beloved, your election of God."

12. 2 peter 1:10 "Wherefore the rather, brethren, give diligence to make your calling and election sure: for if ye do these things, ye shall never fall."

13. Colossians 3:12 " Put on therefore, as the elect of God, holy and beloved, bowels of mercies, kindness, humbleness of mind, meekness, long-suffering."

14. Mark 13:20 "And except that the Lord had shortened those days, no flesh should be saved: but for the elect's sake, whom he hath chosen, he hath shortened the days."

15. Luke 18:7 "And shall not God avenge his own elect, which cry day and night unto him, though he bear long with them?"

16. Matthew 24:22 "And except those days should be shortened, there should no flesh be saved. But for the elect's sake those days shall be shortened."

Scriptures Opposing Predestination

1. John 3:16-18 "For God so loved the world, that he gave his only begotten Son, that whosoever believeth in him should not perish, but have everlasting life. For God sent not his Son into the world to condemn the world; but that the world through him might be saved. He that believeth on him is not condemned; but he that believeth not is condemned already, because he hath not believed in the name of the only begotten Son of God."

2. John 1:11-12 " He came unto his own, and his own received him not, But as many as received him, to them gave he power to become the sons of God, even to them that believe on his name."

3. Romans 1:16 " For I am not ashamed of the gospel of Christ: for it is the power of God unto salvation to every one that believeth; to the Jew first, and also to the Greek."

The doctrine of predestination is stated in the Bible, and the Bible is the inspired word of God, infillable to all intents and purposes. I also support the view that salvation is universally achievable in Christ, by simply believing in Him and in Him along, as one's Lord and personal savior.

M) Some false ides of God

Deism

Webster's Encyclopedic Dictionary, 1941, defines deism as: "[From Latin Deus, God. Deity] One who believes in the existence of a God or supreme being but denies revealed religion, **basing his belief on the light of nature and reason." not "revelation**." All the other religions make claim to special divine revelations and they have requisite "holy" books. Deism has neither.

In Deism there is no need for a preacher, priest or rabbi. All one needs in Deism is his own common sense.

Pantheism

This doctrine holds that everything is God and that the universe and nature are divine. Pantheism is distinguished from panentheism, which holds that God is in everything, but also transcends the Universe. Strict pantheism is not atheism. It does not believe in a transcendent or personal God who is the creator of the universe and the judge of humans. Many pantheists feel the word "God" is too loaded with these connotations and never use the word in their own practice; though they may use it to simplify, or to explain their beliefs to theists about following Christ, not Adam; asserting that what men and women need is moral direction, not a new birth.Therefore, Pelagius saw salvation in purely naturalistic terms-the progress of hum a n nature from sinful behav- ior to holy behav- ior by following the example of Christ.

Stocism

The Stoics were disciples of a Greek philosopher named Zeno. Stoic philosophy is in many ways similar to the Taoist Philosophy of China. Both **teach one to attune with his/her inner nature, which the Romans called Reason, the Chinese the Tao,** and the **Greeks the Logos.** Both encourage simple living and contentment with ones present state of being. **Both view the world as an exchange of opposites**. There are other similarities, which you can explore. Major tenets of Stoism are:

1. One should live in accord with Nature; worldly Nature and human nature.

2. The Unity of All; all gods; all substance; all virtue; all mankind into a Cosmopolis (Universal City)

3. That the external world is maintained by the natural interchange of opposites (poioun/yin, paskhon/yang).

4. That everyone has a personal, individual connection to the All; a god within.

5. That every soul has Free Will to act and that the action of the soul is opinion.

6. Simple Living through moderation and frugality.

7. That spiritual growth comes from seeking the good.

8. That Virtue is the sole good, Vice the sole evil, and everything else indifferent.

9. That the Cardinal Virtues are Prudence, Justice, Fortitude, and Temperance.

10. That the path to personal happiness and inner peace is through the extinguishing of all desire to have or to affect things beyond ones control and through living for the present without hope for or fear of the future; beyond the power of opinion.

Fate or destiny controls everything, whatever will be simply happens and nothing we can do to change things. It is irrational to want that which is not God's will, so attune thyself with thy inner Nature and live happily. Live according to **YOUR own Nature.**

N) Some Pioneering Theologians

Thomas Aquinas (1227-1274)

His classmates originally called him the "dumb ox" because he remained quiet in class. Aquinas subsequently graduated of Notre Dam in Paris, France. He is considered a Doctor of the Catholic Church and patron of Catholic Universities. The greatest work of Thomas Aquinas was the Summa Theological, and it is said to be the fullest presentation of his views. The first part of the Summa is summed up in the thought that God governs the world as the universal first cause. God sways the intellect in that he gives the power to know. About the essence of Angel, Aquinas said that they are not of the same essence of the Father, Son and Holy Spirit, though they are incorporal, intelligent forms, which are not confined to any materal body like man. Angels are not all knowing and not all powerful and not present everywhere like God. On the other hand, man, according to Aquinas, has an essence different from Angels. Man is made of matter and his form or intelligent soul is confined and limited to a body, yet his soul is incorruptible and indestructible, unless God in exercise of His sovereign powers decides to totally destroy both the Forms of man and Angels.

On the question of sin and free will Acquinas said:

"It is manifestly impossible for Him (God) to will the evil of sin; yet He can make choice of one of two opposites, inasmuch as He can will a thing to be, or not to be. In the same way we ourselves, without sin, can will to sit down, and not will to sit down.

"By these signs we name the expression of will by which we are accustomed to show that we will something. A man may show that he wills something, either by himself or by means of another. He may show it by himself, by doing something either directly, or indirectly and accidentally. He shows it directly when he works in his own person; in that way the expression of his will is his own working. He shows it indirectly, by not hindering the doing of a thing; for what removes an impediment is called an accidental mover. In this respect the expression is called permission. A man declares his will by means of another when he orders another to perform a work, either by insisting upon it as necessary by precept, and by prohibiting its contrary; or by persuasion, which is a part of counsel. Since in these ways the will of man makes itself known, the same five are sometimes denominated with regard to the divine will, as the expression of that will. That precept, counsel, and prohibition are called the will of God is clear from the words of Mt. 6:10: "Thy will be done on earth as it is in heaven." That permission and operation are called the will of God is clear from Augustine (Enchiridion 95), who says: "Nothing is done, unless the Almighty wills it to be done, either by permitting it, or by actually doing it."

While receiving his last rites in preparation for death, Aquinas reaffirmed his faith in the Catholic doctrine of Transubstantiation (the communion wine and bread becomes the actual body and blood of Christ when blessed), the essence and substitutionary death of

Christ, in these words:

"If in this world there be any knowledge of this sacrament stronger than that of faith, I wish now to use it in affirming that I firmly believe and know as certain that Jesus Christ, True God and True Man, Son of God and Son of the Virgin Mary, is in this Sacrament ... I receive Thee, the price of my redemption, for Whose love I have watched, studied, and labored. Thee have I preached; Thee have I taught. Never have I said anything against Thee: if anything was not well said, that is to be attributed to my Ignorance. Neither do I wish to be obstinate in my opinions, but if I have written anything erroneous concerning this sacrament or other matters, I submit all to the judgment and correction of the Holy Roman Church, in whose obedience I now pass from this life."

Martin Luther

Luther, a German Catholic Monk, dealt the symbolic blow that began the Reformation, when he nailed his 95 Theses to the door of the Wittenberg Church. That document contained an attack on papal abuses and the sale of indulgences by Catholic Church officials. But Luther himself saw the Reformation as something far more important than a revolt against ecclesiastical abuses. He believed it was a fight for the gospel. Luther even stated that he would have happily yielded every point of dispute to the Pope, if only the Pope had affirmed the gospel. And at the heart of the gospel, in Luther's estimation, was the doctrine of justification by faith—the teaching that Christ's own righteousness is imputed to those who believe, and on that ground alone, they are accepted by God. The fundamental principle of the Reformation, comes from the Apostle Paul's letter to the Romans:"Therefore we conclude that a man is justified by faith without the deeds of the law ..." (Romans 3:28). Therefore, Reformers are Christian Protestants like John Calvin, Ulrich Zwingli, among many others, who followed in the footsteps of Martin Luther in breaking away from the Roman Catholic Church.

Socinians

Faustus Socinus (1539-1604), an Anti-Trinitarian and leader of the Socinians. Socinus maintained that there was only God the Father, a single divine being. The Holy Ghost was not a person but a divine force, not God and not coequal to the Father. Jesus Christ was an exceptional man without sin, but not divine. Salvation required a holy life after the example of the man, Jesus Christ. The Scriptures were the only source of truth.

Arminians

Jacobus Arminius, founder of Arminianism, was born in Holland in 1560. He left Calvinistic Netherlands and went to its base in Geneva, where he was greatly influenced by Beza, who after Calvin's death, assumed Calvin's mantle and took full leadership of the Academy at Geneva. It was Beza who developed the doctrine of predestination a step further than Calvin, in what is known as the supralapsarian view. This has to do with the order of divine decrees. Did God first "decree" election and reprobation (who would be saved and who would be damned) and then permit the fall as a means by which the decree could be carried out (the supralapsarian position, from Latin supra lapsum literally before the fall), or did he first permit that man would fall and then decree election as the method of saving some (infralapsarian from Latin infra lapsus, after the fall)?

The essential dispute that Arminius had with Calvinism regards the doctrine of predestination. He did not deny predestination altogether, but denied that predestination was unconditional. One commendable legacy of Arminius was his call for theological perspective, during a period of intolerant dogmatism, when battle lines were drawn over subtle differences in creeds and confessions. Arminius wrote:

"There does not appear any greater evil in the disputes concerning matters of religion, than the persuading ourselves that our salvation or God's glory are lost by every little difference. As for me, I exhort my scholars, not only to distinguish between the true and the false according to Scripture, but also between the essential articles of faith, and the less essential articles, by the same Scripture."

After Arminius' death, his views were championed and further developed and systematized by two men, Simon Episcopius, and Jan Uytenbogaert. Under their leadership the followers of Arminius in 1610 set forth their views in five articles called

Arminian Articles of Remonstrance, (a remonstrance is a reproof; to remonstrate is to reprove or correct) which gave them the name 'Remonstrants'. In substance the articles teach as follows:

1. God has decreed to save through Jesus Christ those of the fallen and sinful race who through the grace of the Holy Spirit believe in him, but leaves in sin the unbelieving. The

word Predestination is said to be conditioned by God's foreknowledge of who would respond to the gospel).

2. Christ died for all men (not just for the elect), but no one except the believer has remission of sin.

3. Man can neither of himself nor of his free will do anything truly good until he is born again of God, in Christ, through the Holy Spirit. (Though accused of such, Arminius and his followers were not Pelagians.)

4. All good deeds or movements in the regenerate must be ascribed to the grace of God but his grace is not irresistible.

5. Those who are incorporated into Christ by a true faith have power given them through the assisting grace of the Holy Spirit to persevere in the faith. But it is possible for a believer to fall from grace.

Turretin

Francis Turretin was born October 17, 1623. He was a Calvinistic Scholastic Theologian in an age of Protestant, Catholic, Lutheran and Socinian Scholasticism. Like his great predecessor, John Calvin, Turretin entitled his scholastic work Institutio. Turretin said of Scripture " ...We hold it to be necessary simply and absolutely, so that the church can never spare it ... Since God has seen fit for weighty reasons to commit his word to writing. Hence the divine ordination being established, it is made necessary to the church, so that it pertains not only to the well-being (bene esse) of the church, but also to its very existence. Without it the church could not now stand."

So God indeed was not bound to the Scriptures, but he has bound us to them. Although we give to the Scriptures absolute integrity, we do not therefore think that the copyists and printers were inspired (theopneustous), but only that the providence of God watched over the copying of the sacred books, so that although many errors might have crept in, (they have not so crept into the manuscripts) so such errors can be easily corrected by the Scriptures themselves. Therefore, the foundation of the purity and integrity of the sources is not based on fault (anamartesia) of men, but in the providence of God.

Before explaining in many pages several charges of contradictions in Bible passages, Turretin said, " …it will be wiser to acknowledge our own ignorance than to suppose any contradiction."

Epicurus (father of Epicureanism) helped lay the intellectual foundations for modern science and for secular individualism. He established a school in Athens called the "Garden." Epicureans say that all things are self-originated and, so to speak, haphazard. They deny that there is any Mind behind the universe at all. Epicureans deny divine providence and after- life and affirm pleasure as the supreme good of materialistic atomism. They do not recognize the role of divine intelligence in ordering the cosmos. Celsus, an Epicurean wrote: "A True Discourse" which was among the first works to directly challenge the veracity of the Christian scriptures and mock the essential irrationality of many Christian beliefs. Particularly irksome to Christians was his report of a Jewish story that Jesus was not the Son of God, but rather the illegitimate son of a Roman soldier who went by the nickname of "Panther" (the Talmud also describes an illegitimate "Yeshu ben Pandeiros", though he supposedly lived at least a century before the Romans occupied Judea).

Augustine

Augustine was born in Tagaste, Algeria, North Africa, in 354. He was an adherent to Manichaeism, but recommitted himself to Christianity and eventually became a Catholic Monk, and later Bishop of Hippo. He is a pioneering Christian philosopher and educator whose writings inspired such people like Martin Luther, John Calvin and other Protestant Reformers. Prominent among his works are City of God, The Confessions and The Literal Interpretation of Genesis. Augustine taught that human beings, because they are born in original sin, are incapable of saving themselves. Apart from God's grace, it is impossible for a person to obey or even to seek God. Representing the entire race, Adam sinned against God. This resulted in the total corruption of every human being since, so that our very wills are in bondage to our sinful condition. Only God's grace, which he bestows freely as he pleases upon his elect, is credited with the salvation of human beings.

Augustine believed that human kingdoms are established by divine providence. He asserted that if any one attributes their existence to fate, because he calls the will or the power of God itself by the name of fate, let him keep his opinion. Noting that to confess that God exists, and at the same time deny that He has foreknowledge of future things, is the most manifest folly. He insisted that in God's supreme will resides the power which acts on the wills of all created spirits, helping the good, judging the evil, controlling all, granting power to some, not granting it to others. For, as He is the creator of all natures, so also is He the bestower of all powers. Not of all wills; for wicked wills are not from Him, being contrary to nature, which is from Him.

Pelaginism

In sharp contrast, to Augustine, Pelagius was driven by moral concerns and his theology was calculated to provide the most fuel for moral and social improvement. Augustine's emphasis on human helplessness and divine grace would surely paralyze the pursuit of moral improvement, since people could sin with impunity, fatalistically concluding, "I couldn't help it; I'm a sinner." So Pelagius countered by rejecting original sin. According to Pelagius, Adam was merely a bad example, not the father of our sinful condition-we are sinners because we sin-rather than vice versa. Consequently, of course, the Second Adam, Jesus Christ, was a good example. In his Commentary on Romans, Pelagius thought of grace as God's revelation in the Old and New Testaments, which enlightens us and serves to promote our holiness by providing explicit instruction in godliness and many worthy examples to imitate. So human nature is not conceived in sin. After all, the will is not bound by the sinful condition and its affections; choices determine whether one will obey God, and thus be saved.

In 411, Paulinus of Milan came up with a list of six heretical points in the Pelagian message. (1) Adam was created mortal and would have died whether he had sinned or not; (2) the sin of Adam injured himself alone, not the whole human race; (3) newborn children are in the same state in which Adam was before his fall; (4) neither by the death and sin of Adam does the whole human race die, nor will it rise because of the resurrection of Christ; (5) the law as well as the gospel offers entrance to the Kingdom of Heaven; and (6) even before the coming of Christ, there were men wholly without sin. Further, Pelagius and his followers denied unconditional predestination. Anything that falls short of acknowledging original sin, the bondage of the will, and the need for grace to even accept the gift of eternal life, much less to pursue righteousness, is considered by the whole church to be heresy.

The heresy described here is called "Pelagianism.

VI. The Invitation

Friend, Theological Doctrines and the denominations that they have produced do not hold the key to your eternal reconciliation with God, through Jesus His Son. Romans 10: 9 says that if you believe the Lord Jesus in your heart and confess with your mouth that God raised Him from the dead you shall be saved. I now invite you to receive Jesus so your soul can be regenerated or recreated, and you become born again. 2 Corin. 9:17 assures us that if any person is in Christ he is a new creation; the old is past and all things become new. Will you please say this pray and receive Jesus as your personal savior:

This day I, _____, admit that I am a sinner, have broken the laws of God given in the Ten Commandments, and being aware that I cannot save myself, I ask you, Lord Jesus, to forgive me of all my sins (past, present and future), and receive me as your child today. Aman!

You now have no cause to be afraid about the world coming to an end, because Jesus has the entire process in his hands, and He will take very good care of you whatever your situation may be. Come home, come on home friend, Jesus loves you.

Resources

All Scripture references are from The King James Study Bible by Liberty University, 1988

All About God.Com: Gap Theory, No Support.

Clark, R.S. Brief History of Covenant Theology

Constitution of the United States of America

Couch, Mal. An Introduction to Classical Evangelical Hermeneutics, a Guide to the History and practice of Biblical Interpretation-Kregel publication, 2000

Dr. Shower, Renold E. Essay: An Introduction to Dispensational Theology.

Edwards, John. A Complete History or Survey of all the Dispensations.

Flavius Josephus. Jewish War and Antiquities of the Jews.

Geard, Stephen. Essay on Covenant Theology

Huffington Post. Mayan Year 2012 Stirs Apocalpse Predictions, Doomsday, 2009

Katz, Joseph E. The History of the Words "Palestine and Paalestinains.

Kline, Meredith G. Essay: Covenant Theology Under Attack.

Webster Encyclopedic Dictionary, 1941.

Modern, Paul. History Sourcebook: John Calvin on Predestination June 1998.

National Geographic Daily News Article: Shroud of Turin Not Jesus' by Mati Milstein, December 2010.

Poiret, Pierr.The Divine Economy: A Universal System of the Works and purposes of God Towards Men Demonstrated, 1687